Initiation into
DREAM
MYSTERIES

"Sarah Janes's *Initiation into Dream Mysteries* reads like a perfect dream. Not only through the vivid reanimation of the dream cults of antiquity but also through the mellifluous prose by which it is brought to life, the reader (or initiate) is taken on a special journey—as intellectually insightful as it is spiritually inspiring. The text is the synergy of a depth of knowledge and love for the world—mingled with the initiatory stories interspliced throughout, hypnotically elaborate and evocative—that will lift you up to taste that same awakening that was the intent of these very oneiric practices of old."

PASCAL MICHAEL, LECTURER ON PSYCHEDELICS,
ALTERED STATES, AND TRANSPERSONAL
PSYCHOLOGY AT ALEF TRUST

Initiation into
DREAM
MYSTERIES

Drinking from the
Pool of Mnemosyne

A Sacred Planet Book

SARAH JANES

Destiny Books
Rochester, Vermont

Destiny Books
One Park Street
Rochester, Vermont 05767
www.DestinyBooks.com

Text stock is SFI certified

Destiny Books is a division of Inner Traditions International

Sacred Planet Books are curated by Richard Grossinger, Inner Traditions editorial board member and cofounder and former publisher of North Atlantic Books. The Sacred Planet collection, published under the umbrella of the Inner Traditions family of imprints, includes works on the themes of consciousness, cosmology, alternative medicine, dreams, climate, permaculture, alchemy, shamanic studies, oracles, astrology, crystals, hyperobjects, locutions, and subtle bodies.

Cataloging-in-Publication Data for this title is available from the Library of Congress

ISBN 978-1-64411-514-5 (print)
ISBN 978-1-64411-515-2 (ebook)

Printed and bound in the United States by Lake Book Manufacturing, LLC. The text stock is SFI certified. The Sustainable Forestry Initiative® program promotes sustainable forest management.

10 9 8 7 6 5 4 3 2 1

Text design by Kenleigh Manseau
This book was typeset in Garamond Premier Pro with Spirits Soft used as the display typeface
Artwork by Sarah Janes

To send correspondence to the author of this book, mail a first-class letter to the author c/o Inner Traditions • Bear & Company, One Park Street, Rochester, VT 05767, and we will forward the communication, or contact the author directly at **themysteries.org**.

For my beloved, wonderful, patient, sensible, healthy, happy, and hilarious daughter Indi.

Contents

The Dream Initiation

∞∞C

Acknowledgments

To the divine and sublime Pascal Immanuel Michael. Thank you for all the deep-feeling, brain-tingling conversations, life-affirming kindred spirit-ness, culturally enriching outings, and 1980s "psi"-fi critiquing fun company. Your invested read-throughs, your sensible ἐνθουσιασμός, your dream revelations are cherished. Your neuroscience-speak checks have been very much appreciated. You will never die. You're my Spitzberger!

With deep appreciation to Richard Grossinger, Patricia Rydle, Erica Robinson, Jeanie Levitan, Albo Sudekum, Margaret Jones, and everyone at Inner Traditions for making this book a reality. To my fellow conspirator, Grecophile, and dear friend Anthony Peake—thank you so much for your ongoing encouragement, involvement, and interest in my work. Your indefatigable curiosity and energy is an inspiration to me.

With much gratitude to Ioannis Leventis of Kaktos Publications in Athens—for future memories of dream festivals and reactivated sleep temples in Greece.

With love to my friends for their endless support, faith, and excellent sense of humor, especially Maya Evans, Jennie Howell, Erika Holland, Rosanna Lowe, Thilaka Hillman, Claudia Barton, Jakki Pransky, Elise Heywood, Ingrid Pryer, Tim Scullion, Susan McNally, and Charles Holmes. My gratitude and thanks to everyone who has ever come to one of my talks or workshops.

I am so grateful for Mum and Dad's mantra: "Everyone hates their job, Sarah!" So thank you, Bev and Dave, for inspiring me to never get a proper job.

Thank you to Miss Pussycat and Quintron of New Orleans for keeping the faith and always being the most fun, inspiring, generous, joyful, and creative friends in the world. Thank you so much for all of the adventures. There is nothing better in the world than having a laugh with your mates. I hope this book sells millions of copies so that I can take you on a luxurious European spa bender.

Thank you to Carl Hayden Smith for providing endless fun projects, adventures, and nonstop high vibes. To DB for one year of domestic, rock-solid, mock-fueled bliss.

My heartfelt thanks to the many experts and academics I have had the pleasure to meet, talk to, or correspond with over the course of my research, and from whom I have learned so very much. In particular, David Luke, Tim Read, Rupert Sheldrake, Guy Hayward, Jose Montemayor Alba, Egyptologists and ancient dream text experts Kasia Szpakowska and Luigi Prada, Lucia Gahlin, Anne Austin, Gregory Shushan, Aidan Dodson, Salima Ikram, Angela Voss, Campbell Price, Dallas Campbell, Dora Goldsmith, Sofia Aziz, Paul Harrison, John J. Johnston, Danny Nemu, Sam Gandy, Alistair Coombs, Mark A. Schroll, Ryan Hurd, Jade Shaw, David Bramwell, Chris Naunton, Joanne Backhouse, Eva Voutsaki, Craig Sams, Gregory Sams, Engelbert Winkler, Dirk Proeckl, Ann Mathie, Darren Springer, Blay Whitby, Miguel Alexiades, Birger Ekornåsvåg Helgestad, Irving Finkel, Brian Earp, my Mesopotamian spiritual guru Vanessa Lavallée, Jay Silverstein, Samantha Treasure, Gary Lachman, Mervat Nasser, Ramadan B. Hussein (may your *ba* soar in Heaven), Matt Brown, Andreas Kornevall, Errol Fuller, Alexandra Stein, Adam Malone, Luciana Haill, Akal Anand Kaur, Maria Papaspyrou, Maria Almena, Adah Parris, Sasha Frost, Tree Carr, Pablo Bueno Melchor, Matteo Zamagni, Lena Korkovelou, Rebecca Sharrock, Caz Coronel, Emma McCann, Jason Fité, Alan Roberts, Matt Harvey, Diane Powell, Steve Taylor, Graham Nicholls, Jim Elvidge, Susan Demeter, Daniel Abella, Mary Fahl, Peter Broughan, Neil Rushton, Myron Dyal, Leo Ruickbie, Imants Baruss, Stanley Krippner, Rosalind Park, Hana Navratilova, James D. Rietveld, Lee Gerrard-Barlow, Daniel Oldis, Thomas Sheridan, Katie Holland, Amanda Mariamne Radcliffe, William Rowlandson, and for his invaluable and extraordinarily thorough research into the incubatory practices and dream institutions of antiquity, Gil Renberg.

Special thanks and love to my amazing and creative daughter Indiana Joy Janes, for making me do the work, for being so wholesome, and for having such an excellent sense of humor. With much love to my adorable nieces and nephews: George, Jack, Meri, Pinja, Harry, and Jake, and my extra kids by another mutha, Ruby and Frank Holland.

Keep it in the vortex forever!

I had a dream that I was healed by a woman, a living Venus of Willendorf. In a green garden, she rolled her warm flesh all over my body and was perfumed with rare oils and crushed grasses. She told me that she sent healing through my bones, and it felt incredible. Spring exploded within me. Then she took me into her home. We went through her father's bedroom, and he was very old. He had vitiligo and was in bed. She told me that she would take over as chief, once he died.

MARCH 22, 2022

Introduction
Ka, the Creative Spirit
Dreaming, Memory, and Consciousness

The power that drives the looping plasma of the sun, that throws asteroids at the moon, this is the power that inspires creation. The pattern of creation expresses itself through the branches of trees as they stretch up to adore the heavens. It shines through the whorl of a murex shell cast on a beach. It spirals out of the radiant cores of sunflowers and cabbages. Divine order is inscribed on our own human bodies, through our swirling fingerprints and the convolutions of our hearts. It is hidden in the folds and fireworks of our brains. The language of the world can be heard in the murmur of streams, in the wind as it dances through the leaves of a forest canopy and in the exultation of birds at dawn. In the wordless rhythm of glints upon a restless sea, the world speaks.

From the center of our planet, a divine force emanates into the universe, interacting with the other forces of creation. In this cosmic play, we tremble like beads of dew on a spider's web. We are singular but connected; we absorb the All as water, and we reflect the All like a mirror.

The force of consciousness ebbs and flows as a magnetic tide. When it is strong, humans feel it as something divine and rapturous. It becomes enough to be alive for even a second in this incredible Eden. A sunrise can make a human collapse in awe. The language of solar light speaks

1

directly to the *ka,* the divine human spark, as conceptualized by ancient Egyptian people. The ka is that portion of the divine contained within every living body; it resides in the heart. The ka animates us during our lifetime and returns us to the All when our mortal body perishes. The ancient Egyptians recognized a variety of material and immaterial forms of an individual, the most significant soul aspects being the *ka* ⊔ and *ba* 𓅡. The ka in a sense is *will,* the animating force of life, the creative principle and vital essence. The ba—represented by a human-headed bird—is the individual soul, the personality, and was seen to have a unique mobile agency following bodily death.

The hieroglyph that depicts the ka, ⊔, is a natural posture of adoration and worship in many ancient cultures. It shows arms upraised and framing the heart, projecting the divine spark of the soul into the universe and allowing the All to flow into a person, who acts as a vessel. The heart 𓄣 (*ib*) in the ancient Egyptian language), is represented by a stylized heart-shaped pot, and to feel love or joy or bliss is to be inebriated, heart brimming over with the elixir of happiness. It is noteworthy that many later religions bring the hands together in front of the heart to pray, almost as though one were symbolically shutting the gate on divine cosmic connection and influence and making the universe a little smaller and more personal by closing the human circuit.

When the force of cosmic consciousness is weak, when we are cut off from the divine dimension of life, humans become confused. We contrive ever new, complex, artificial ways to seek joy, to give life value, and to find some meaning within it.

It is much easier to feel the subtle powers of creation when immersed in nature. The qualia, the individual experiences of subjective, conscious experience, can intermix with the qualia of nature. The patterns found in nature are expressions of cosmic consciousness. The threads of Heaven and Earth weave together to make up the human fabric. It can be said with certainty that not a single soul on their deathbed will ever say, "I wish I had spent more time online," or even, "I wish I had bought more stuff." So it is advisable and good to be in the natural elements, to learn to truly love and adore nature. There is no secret to the universe; the universe is inherently divine.

○ ○ ○

In this precise, present moment and for all eternity you exist as part of a divine, conscious, mysterious, universe full of magic. From my ka to your ka, thank you for reading my book.

○ ○ ○

THE POTENCY OF THE PRESENT

Over time, the invention of art, games, religion, building, and language have created a separation between nature and us humans, even as these aspects of human life were originally conceived to encode the divine laws of natural order. Long ago, religious myths in particular were contrived to strengthen the relationship between humans and the cosmos, between humans and the cycle of creation.

As our species has increasingly removed itself from the matrix of nature, the religious myths of our ancestors have fragmented into hierarchy, dogma, and routine. We no longer recognize the astronomical and agrarian wisdom they were written to encode. As we have invented ever more elaborate technologies and scientific disciplines to make sense of our world, we find ourselves inhabiting increasingly complex layers of abstraction and getting caught up in those details. The greater *mystery* is always hidden in plain sight; it is only the nature of our perception, appreciation, and attention that has shifted.

When you have music on in the background, you are not *really* listening to music. A deep listening experience feels entirely different. We have the universe on in the background all of the time. To tap in to divine cosmic consciousness, to truly appreciate our life, we can choose to give it our full attention at times. We need to listen deeply and become engrossed and enraptured. Our attention augments our perception of the world, and it is our appreciation and adoration that can glorify the world and our experience of it. We might try to return to the same sort of mode of appreciation we had as children. To experience divinity, we need to stop, slow down, and fully engage with the present moment. A fingerprint of eternity dwells within every truly present moment. The reality of a timeless, immortal consciousness can be experienced in a truly present moment of bliss. This is something that we can experience powerfully in the lucid dream state.

LIFE PATTERNS AND POWERS

The planetary power of Earth, Earth's magnetosphere, is in constant flux. Is it possible that our ancestors had more developed and integrated senses for magnetoreception, and did this somehow influence their consciousness and perception of reality?[1]

Magnetoreception is a sense found across many diverse species, and humans possess at least some of the biochemical requirements, enabling them to respond to the inherent rhythms of nature and Gaia. For example, the cryptochrome protein (CRY2), a flavoprotein in the eye, is a blue-light receptor and plays a critical role in circadian rhythm generation.[2]

Human form and consciousness calibrate in patterns of coherence and interference. As biological forms take shape, they respond to the electromagnetic forces of both the local and cosmic environment that surrounds them. Cosmic emanations blossom like divine breaths, hidden within space. Their rhythms and languages are concealed from humanity by their sheer enormity. The waves and pulses of multitudinous cosmic influences and the rippling, magnetic aura of our own home planet have interacted for aeons. These forces shaped our planet and continue to give birth to life on Earth. They orchestrate the interweaving landscapes of life and death. When our physical bodies finally relinquish their divine spark, we might perhaps discover there is a black hole at the center of our souls. Maybe we travel through this black hole when we die . . .

Between the immeasurably small and beyond the immeasurably massive, there might exist something like a synaptic gap in space and time. So perhaps when we take this electrical leap of faith, we will find ourselves passing through a timeless dimension, our memories obliterated by the journey. We might pop out of an abyss and find ourselves in another reality. In this other reality we might find ourselves ready to live another life, or perhaps we will live the same lives over and over again.

Near-death experiences can illustrate the profoundly transformative and healing potential of reflecting on the immortal and, even more importantly, of having a direct, transcendent experience of the divine, whatever that is.

But what if our ideas about the afterlife are merely a creative product of our living thoughts, experiences, and emotions? For a meaningful and pleasurable life, it probably still makes good sense to invest in the very best thoughts, emotions, and experiences whenever possible. Do we have to believe in something?

We are all connected to our most distant ancestors, and we are already incubating our descending influences. Strip away all the artifice of modern life, and we exist in a spectacularly divine moment of creation.

WHERE DO DREAMS COME FROM?

We cannot speak of dreams without also talking about creativity, consciousness, divination, prophecy, magic, medicine, religion, the soul, stars, and death. The cultures that developed around dreaming are intimately interwoven with ancient spiritual perceptions of reality, animistic traditions, and otherworld beliefs.

Dream themes reoccur and are maintained from deepest antiquity right up to the present day. Ancient high cultures that were steeped in a rich, mythic landscape of gods and goddesses, storytellers and symbolism, had their mythology writ large. For those of us living in the modern era, we explore our personal mythology in dreams and the confused narratives of childhood TV shows, contemporary media, and the internet. Models of creation, interpretations of reality are the products of culture and the prevailing mediums. Many of the first creation myths had humans crafted out of clay; today philosophers talk about simulation theory. We are still bombarded with mythology, however. The stories and classical archetypes of the ancients still influence us. We might lack some of the cohesion and conciseness that must have existed in the sort of mythic cognition possessed by our ancestors, but the same archetypes continue to ride roughshod through our imaginations, and they still attempt to reveal us to ourselves—whether or not we want them to.

○ ○ ○

Some dreams have special powers. Some dreams can fill you with awe and bliss, alter your perspective, open your mind, and enable you to connect with feelings beyond your ordinary perceptual and sensory capabilities.

This book is structured to work as an initiation, one that is self-generated and ultimately guided by you, the reader. It will take you on an imaginal journey somewhat in the spirit of the Mystery Schools of antiquity. The psychomagic narratives and guided hypnagogic meditations in this book will help you integrate transformative and archetypal imagery into your own dreams, for healing purposes.

The dream avatars you meet throughout this journey will be your Creatrix, your Hierophant, and your Healer. They have always been there, but magical language, myth, story, and alchemical imagery can inspire lucid dreams, and in such dreams you can access your latent powers.

The initiates of the great ancient Mystery Schools of antiquity, of Eleusis, Samothrace; of Dionysus, Osiris and Isis, Mithra, and so on, were said to return from their experiences no longer afraid of death. Having tasted the immortal reality of divine truth, they lived richer, more fulfilling lives, and they found a deeper appreciation for themselves and the reality of which they were a part. The word *mystery* is derived from the Greek verb *myein,* "to close," as in the eyes and mouth. Secrecy is frequently a vital part of ancient magic. To reveal the particulars of the initiatory rites to any uninitiated person was unthinkable and even punishable by death under certain circumstances.

In our current age, most everything feels knowable, or at least accessible. The mysteries inside and outside ourselves are being systematically picked apart, uncovered, and revealed. We think we know, or are at least capable of finding out, everything about everything. Our technologies and media enable us to see crystal-clear images of the cosmos on a daily basis—of extremely distant planets, foreign people, and strange new lands and the minutiae of their exotic flora and fauna.

Think of mystery as one of our senses. As a sense, it is a delectable component of conscious contemplation, one that provides much wonderment, awe, and delight. Mystery activates the imagination, it provokes and electrifies our spirit, it is the poetry of life, the shadow within the prose of the *known*. As human beings, we are not just seeking knowledge, information, or even meaning. We want rapture; we crave cosmic connection; we love joy; we need to adore something.

Perhaps the last mystery that remains to us is the lived experience of death. What happens in those final moments, when our personal embodied experience as a living, breathing human being evaporates? This is perhaps life's true initiation in pure mystery. If we can remember ourselves in dreams, if we can make our own dreaming into a conscious art, can we perhaps navigate more mindfully into this unknown? Can we cross the threshold and not forget ourselves?

Invocation of Mnemosyne

I invoke Mnemosyne, Greek goddess and Titaness—personification of memory, of remembrance, guardian of the waters of memory, and lady of divine eloquence. Daughter of Heaven, *Ouranos*, and Earth, *Gaia*, mother of inspiration, source of the nine Muses and psychopomp of the Orphic Mysteries. You—enthroned, sense-making queen of the Dark Oracle of Trophonius—Mnemosyne, you are my muse. May your blessings permeate each page of this book.

Mnemosyne was often the last deity invoked in the dream incubation rituals of the sleep sanctuaries of ancient Greece. Such ancient wisdom invites us to learn more about our own memory and consciousness, by studying and remembering ourselves in dreams.

As part of your own dreaming rituals you might like to invoke the spirit of the goddess Mnemosyne to strengthen and vivify your powers of memory. The Orphic Hymn to Mnemosyne below instructs the dream seeker to honor the goddess with a fumigation of frankincense. The mildly psychoactive properties of frankincense smoke enable memories to be colorfully recalled. Frankincense is also known to alleviate anxiety and depression, so it's a very useful ally for dreamwork. In Arabian and African mythology, the frankincense tree (*Boswellia sacra*) is a petrified female lover, a daughter of the jinn (supernatural spirits of Arabian folklore) who fell in love with a human boy. Her fragrant, lovelorn tears are crystallized droplets of grief, and when cast onto hot coals they transmute into a heart-healing medicine, a holy sacrament for the people. The ninth-century Persian chronicler al-Tabari wrote, "The smoke of incense reaches heaven as does no other smoke."

Fumigation from Frankincense

The consort I invoke of Zeus divine, source of the holy,
    sweetly speaking Nine;
Free from th' oblivion of the fallen mind, by whom the soul
    with intellect is join'd:
Reason's increase, and thought to thee belong, all-powerful,
    pleasant, vigilant, and strong:
'Tis thine, to waken from lethargic rest all thoughts deposited
    within the breast;
And nought neglecting, vigorous to excite the mental eye
    from dark oblivion's night.
Come, blessed power, thy mystic's mem'ry wake to holy rites,
    and Lethe's fetters break.

LXXVI ORPHIC HYMN TO MNEMOSYNE,
TRANSLATED BY THOMAS TAYLOR

It is unfortunate that in the West we have historically not integrated more of the rich wisdom developed over millennia by our ancestors. Yet within the Western psyche, a certain appetite remains for transcendental experience, the desire to see the spiritual dimension of life. This is what leads so many seekers of the ineffable to the spiritual doctrines and meditation technologies of the East. It could be argued that a parallel Western occult tradition was disrupted during the Bronze Age collapse, which saw the cataclysmic disintegration and complete societal breakdown of a number of high cultures. Complex civilizations, from

Anatolia (modern-day Turkey) and the Near East, through Greece, Egypt, and across the Levant, were systematically razed, their cultural legacies decimated. Previously well-organized and educated populations were reduced to pockets of subsistence survivalists with dwindling literacy.

I'm inclined to think that in our current Dark Age we are still feeling the aftereffects, both intellectually and culturally, of that devastation. In this book I present some of what has been discovered about the ancient dream arts, philosophies, and incubation techniques of this esoteric lineage. I do so in the hope that modern dreamers might extract maximum benefit from their mysterious and enigmatic dream journeys. Hopefully this book will help you learn more about your own inner imaginal landscape and enable you to cultivate continuity with the dreamings of those who dreamed this weird world into existence many thousands of years ago.

On the subject of ancestors, I have always found museums to be reassuring sanctuaries that illustrate the incredible potential of the human species (weapons and war galleries aside) to appreciate and glorify the natural world. I would like to put forward the idea that museums and certain archaeological sites are ideal places for modern dream incubation. The hallowed galleries of a museum offer us space to honor and an opportunity to understand our ancestors. The Greek root of the word museum is *mousa*, "muse." A muse divinely inspires and provokes excellent thinking. We should make it our business to learn all we can about history, as history really serves as humanity's collective memory. With clear knowledge, an understanding of history, and lucid memories, we have wisdom, and with wisdom we can make the best possible decisions about the future.

Countless collections of ancient artifacts in museums all over the world allude to a deep connection among ancient peoples, the stars, landscapes, and other species. The further back we go, the deeper these connections appear to be. Many of these objects hint at the fact that ancient people viewed themselves, reality, the heavens, our planet, and all of its life-forms as a dynamic, interconnected, intelligent entity. Earth worship remains a thoroughly legitimate spiritual practice that is worth returning to. Earth *is* a living entity; we depend on the health of Earth for our survival, and we of course thrive when Earth thrives. When our environment is healthy and beautiful, we beautify ourselves. Our role as human beings is to create Heaven on Earth. To adore and nourish the land we live on, to cultivate its incredible artistry, to make it lovely, fecund, abundant, and biodiverse is to respect, nurture, and cherish ourselves. We honor our ancestors and provide for our descendants when we care for the Earth. Conceivably, we could all turn our attention toward making this planet the most fantastic, paradisal, life-enhancing place imaginable, a harmonious garden that gives joy, pleasure, shade, vibrant color, living water, eyeball dissolving beauty, luscious produce, and sweet dreams to all of its inhabitants.

LUCID DREAMING

A lucid dream is a dream in which you can remember who and where you are. Scientifically speaking, it is an altered dream state whereby a dreamer displays levels of higher-order consciousness, something not seen in ordinary dreams. It is a hybrid state of consciousness with a neural signature made up of both REM sleep and wakefulness features. Lucid dreamers demonstrate metacognition, the ability to think about thinking, *within* a dream.

The neural basis of this meta-insight appears to be activation of the right dorsolateral prefrontal cortex and the precuneus, regions that are more or less dormant (showing low regional cerebral blood flow) during ordinary REM sleep.[3] These brain areas are associated with memory, self-assessment and perception, visuospatial processing, and decision making. Frequent lucid dreamers in real life are very often excellent problem solvers. MRI scans of the brains of regular lucid dreamers show that they consistently have more gray matter and increased functional connectivity between the frontopolar cortex and temporoparietal association areas.[4]

At its best, the lucid dream experience is utterly ecstatic and awe inspiring, but this aspect of the phenomenon is rather understudied. As is also evident in psychedelic trip reports, the veracity of epiphanies received in a lucid dream can feel intensely, overwhelmingly meaningful in the moment but upon reflection might be rather nonsensical or vague.[5] I suspect that a particularly activated brain state in a lucid dream kickstarts the visual cortex to generate visual content that matches an ecstatic feeling, likely through association-based reconstructions of the sort of visual impressions that accompanied previously experienced ecstatic feelings. On a more philosophical note, what if this ecstasy is an embodied remembrance of primal timelessness and immaterial reality, a momentary return to our divine source?

A more humdrum example of this sort of cognitive mismatch between feeling and meaning might be seen in the lucid dream *joke,* which in the dream has you crying with laughter for what seems like eternity, but upon awakening you realize that the joke was not remotely funny at all. Despite this, it is my belief that a lucid experience of embodied bliss has real-life agency to activate transformation and self-healing.

The lucid experience is rich, deeply involved, creative, and often ecstatic. So perhaps it is this ecstasy that is the elixir, the medicine, the inner alchemy. Memories reworked in dreams often have an emotional core, and regulation of emotions certainly seems to be another important psychological function of the dreaming experience.[6] We are emotional creatures. Our inner dialogue sculpts our emotional state and therefore directs our dream experiences.

In lucid dreams, you become viscerally aware of the fact that as the dreamer you are the progenitor of your dream world. You know you are not just the dream avatar but the entire multidimensional fabric of the dream reality. This can sometimes enable you to change and manifest objects, locations, characters, and scenarios at will. It allows for a feeling of omniscience. Could repeated episodes of lucidity then somehow promote neurogenesis and contribute to increased neural connectivity? Specifically, would frequent activation of the prefrontal cortex during lucid dream states encourage connectivity to develop over time via frequently activated, uniquely lucid neural pathways? Or conversely, do brains wired this way in the first instance make one predisposed to lucid dreaming?

The supernatural and omnipotent feelings that regularly occur in lucid dreams make me wonder if such experiences inspired original ideas about divine beings with magical powers—the gods. Things like flight, telepathy, future vision, power over animals, morphing into new forms, immense strength and control of the elements, for example, are regular features of the lucid dream landscape and are skills frequently attributed to the earliest gods. Similarly, did dreams inspire the first stories, being as they are often composed of many of the aforementioned peculiarities and usually involving a journey? Dreams tend to have a questing aspect to them and are rarely stationary.

I have been a lucid dreamer since childhood. My entire life has been guided by an enthusiasm for dreaming and the dream aesthetic. In particular I am fascinated by the uniquely expanded awareness offered by the lucid dream state. Several recent scientific studies into the altered states activated by psychedelics,[7] near-death experiences, and even real death experiences are now identifying neurophysiological markers that parallel those seen in the lucid dream–experiencing brain.[8] As a child, my intuition told me that lucid dreaming offered an opportunity to expand the human experience and transcend the mortal realm. Through my research over the past couple of decades I have come to the conclusion that this is a view that was shared and celebrated by our most distant ancestors around the globe.

WHAT IS DREAM INCUBATION?

Put simply, dream incubation is any technique or combination of techniques aimed at engendering a desired dream. For our ancestors this would most likely involve seeking out a divine entity or deceased person. This being might offer insight into the future, counsel, a miracle, a cure, or a spontaneous divine healing. Traditionally, dream incubation preparatory rituals usually involved a combination of purging, catharsis, fasting, purification, sacrifice, offerings, prayer, magical writing and charms, pilgrimage to sacred sites, and sometimes dream induction via certain oneirogenic substances. Across Mesopotamia, the Levant, ancient Egypt, and Greece, combinations of all of these techniques were employed. The dream practices of cultures such as these—ones with advanced writing and recording systems as well as schools for elite priestly scribes—most certainly developed through the metaphysical lens of the nonliterate cultures that predate them. The idea of making oneself "pure" is a sort of pagan precursor to the slogan "cleanliness is next to godliness." By turning yourself into a clean and pure vessel, you bring yourself into alignment with the divine principle and invite holy favor.

As well, the influence of language and early writing on dreaming cannot be overstated. Writing is itself a magical act, and many ancient scripts evolved out of symbolic art and pictographic forms. As dream interpretation developed into a profession in ancient Near Eastern civilizations, it gives the appearance of being seen as a job primarily for the literate. Wordplay, punning, especially homophones—hinting at its nonliterate roots—and association are the mainstays of classical dream interpretation texts in ancient Egypt, for example.[9] I believe that human spiritual thought, and therefore many of our world's cultures, gestated in a nexus of memory, language, and dreams.

Language programs our cultural memory and is fine-tuned in the consolidating processes of dreaming. Each night we reconfigure ourselves according to our world and reaffirm to ourselves who we are, where we are, and what our story is. So perhaps another way to look at dreams is to see that they provide an incubation realm for personality, a liminal zone in which the architecture of the psyche can evolve. Maybe this is why babies spend about 50 percent of their time in memory-organizing REM sleep—twice as much time as adults do.[10] Perhaps in these luxuriously long REM sleep phases babies are working extra hard to figure out who they are, where they are, and what their story is.

DREAMTIME AS A MIRROR REALM

The dream realm has a hall-of-mirrors quality to it. In dreams we are able to see ourselves from multiple perspectives; we become all eyes, examining self from every angle. In ordinary consciousness it *seems* as though we exist as an independent entity. We occupy a sort of liminal state in which we have learned to peel our individual identity away from the rest of the cosmos. On the hidden side of the thin, reflective layer that is the awake I is the otherworld of *dream us*—a fractalized I, a shuffling self-image, eternally seeking some sort of coherence.

In the nascent field of geopsychology, studies have shown that personality traits can form in response to all sorts of external factors, including geology, weather, environment, landscape, and local culture.[11] I believe we integrate this vast amount of data most intensively at night, slowly constructing our own inner mirror realm over a lifetime and using it as a space to organize and reconcile the experiences we have of the waking world. That this mirror realm might also enable one to access the collective consciousness or that it appears to many as an alternate, etheric-type of reality or dimension are particularly intriguing ideas that we shall explore in more detail throughout this book.

Have you ever had the experience of rousing from sleep and suddenly not knowing who or where you are? It feels as though for a moment your entire identity is in suspension. Experiences such as this, a sort of parasomnia, or confused arousal experience,[12] most commonly experienced by small children, make me wonder where exactly it is that our dreams take shape and play out. Dreams and sleep clearly have extraordinarily important roles in memory-making and consciousness, but the complete system remains imperfectly understood.

I wonder if the ancients, with their reverence for memory, ancestors, and the sophisticated mnemonic devices they developed for their oral storytelling traditions, had different, perhaps more entangled conscious and subconscious memory-processing faculties than us contemporary humans. Humans nowadays seem to have outsourced much of their memory to the digital storage structures within the synthetic global brain of the all-pervasive internet. This universal neural network now appears to be orchestrating most of our lives. It has put something of a dent into our ability to remember and imagine, and this has manifested in what is known as digital amnesia or digital dementia[13] and might even be a contributing factor in some cases of aphantasia, the inability to form mental images of people, places, and things.[14] Without coherent personal memories and a vibrant imagination, can we have good dream lives? Without good dream lives, what kind of waking lives do we lead? Many children have wonderful dream lives with many incidents of lucidity. Alongside other neurophysiological features of the youthful brain, much of this might be attributed to the amount of time young children spend in imaginative play.

ANCIENT DREAM ORACLES

In the ancient world, a dream oracle might have referred to a person—a professional dreamer, one who dreams on your behalf and predicts your future for you—or it could be one's own prophetic dream, in which the future is revealed, usually by cryptic signs that might be further teased out by a dream interpreter. In ancient records, a dream of the future is rarely described as being a straightforward vision of events yet to unfold; it is more likely to resemble a kind of visual puzzle composed of dream signs, often visual representations of a word or words, that with expert rearrangement can come to write out the essential elements of the prediction.

The oracular nature of dreaming throughout the ancient world really fascinates me. I think it demonstrates that the human being functions as a prediction generator and sense maker, perhaps as a result of the unique niche we have come to occupy within the animal kingdom. The development of art, games, architecture, and language gave us tools to represent the world as we saw it, and in doing so we came to create an imaginal, mental layer of reality, one of information, thoughts, ideas, and possibilities, very much like the concept of the noosphere as elucidated by Vladimir Vernadsky and Pierre Teilhard de Chardin. Even in our information-rich age—and paradoxically, considering our science-led culture—we seem to be returning to something of an oracular mind-set. We modern people are increasingly overwhelmed and saturated with information, and as we desperately seek to find meaning, to make sense of it all, we disassociate. Our consciousness appears to fragment as it attempts to predict the future in an increasingly complex, furiously fast-changing and chaotic world.

Our salvation is where it has always been—in deep connection with nature and transcendent, rapturous experience.

THE APPROACH OF THIS BOOK

This book serves as an initiation. How can a book initiate a reader? Reading is known to have certain consciousness-altering effects. Books impart knowledge in a personal and particular way, and fiction especially can take a reader on an imagined adventure in a created world. A reader is capable of feeling deep compassion, empathy, or loathing for a fictional character. Most of us have some favorite books, and when we remember these books we often remember them visually, as if we ourselves have lived these stories somehow, somewhere.

This book is designed as a psychomagic journey, one that will take you on a quest to explore your own narrative and help you connect with the divine reverberations of your own distant-dreaming ancestors. In the story sections I've purposefully used language, repetition, double-meaning, and symbols that are inspired by ancient dream texts. My intention is to encourage you to inculcate dreaming metacognition—an awareness and understanding of one's own thought processes from *within* a dream. I trust that this will help you construct your own mythic mise-en-scène. As we travel through the different time periods explored in this book, it is my intention that each stage of this initiation, each phase, as I have called the chapters, will take you closer to full dream gnosis.

This book is part nonfiction and part fiction. The mythic history of our ancestors shows us over and over again that wisdom, about the self and the other, can be reliably encoded and transmitted through stories. It is possible, in fact, that the first-ever stories were born in dreams.

Why stories? It is often easier to remember information when it is delivered using drama or personalized narrative. A story can have beauty and powerful imagery. When information engages the senses and emotions, it sinks in more deeply. Beyond this, as humans, we have the unique ability to work stories into our lives. We empathize with fantasy characters; we are able *see* through their eyes and *feel* through their senses.

With our fantastic, often underrated imaginal abilities—abilities no doubt advanced over millennia through myth and story—we can really live imaginatively though fiction. This is supported by neuroscience, which has discovered that when we read stories, neural pathways form in response to the world and experiences they describe.[15] We conjure these worlds, we dream about them. A story is a co-creative process, a dynamic between the world-building imaginings of the author and the active imagination of the reader. We are inherently creative beings, and thus stories will always appeal to us because they help us make sense of our lives.

Each phase, or chapter, of this book explores a different era and is followed by a story. The stories are an opportunity for the subconscious mind to engage more deeply and intuitively with the cultural narratives of the time period in question. These stories came to me in my dreams, in response to my own dream incubation sessions and requested visions for writing this book. As these stories are made out of my own dream material, it is my hope that they will inspire your dreaming, as the dream aesthetic tends to inspire more of the same.

I am indebted to the format of the ancient Mystery festival, such as that found in the Mysteries of Eleusis.[16] I think it is very likely that the ritual dramas and sacred rites that took place in the Telesterion, the ultimate initiation hall of the ancient pan-Hellenic Eleusinian Mysteries, were most deeply integrated and worked into personal epiphanies in the dreams that followed the neophyte's real-life experience. I have noticed that in my own dreams, when I have been inspired by spectacle or observed drama, I become the protagonist of dream reconstructions.

ABOUT THE AUDIO RECORDINGS

This book is accompanied by a seven-part guided hypnagogic journey. Each audio recording serves as a complement to a narrative chapter, and together the story and sound act as a stage in the self-initiatory process. The individual recordings each require about forty-five minutes of listening time, and I suggest creating a sacred space within your home or out in nature that is dedicated to your private dream incubation rituals.

It is worth creating a serene and relaxing environment in which distractions and outside noise can be minimized easily, and basic sleep hygiene protocol followed. You can find the transcripts for these meditations in a supplemental chapter at the end of the book. The audio recordings are available for download at

audio.innertraditions.com/InDrMy

Tips for Dream Incubation

- Perform your dream incubation during the day when possible. Lucid dreaming often occurs during afternoon naps, and you are more likely to remember your hypnagogic reverie if you do incubation during the day. Setting a regular time for your incubation session might make it easier to achieve the right state of mind.
- Create a safe, relaxing, calm space in which to incubate.
- Turn all of your devices off and have as little light as possible near you.
- Lie on your back; you are less likely to fall into a deep sleep if you lie in this position.
- You might also like to choose an essential oil or scent to accompany your rituals. Olfaction plays a special role in emotional memory formation and retrieval.
- Be clean and warm.
- When you begin to visualize things, keep in mind that you need to keep moving forward through the dreamscape and into full dream consciousness. Hypnagogia is very much like Alice falling down the rabbit hole before she gets to Wonderland; keep a soft gaze, allowing the visuals to flow past you.
- For many people, fasting seems to produce vivid dreams and echoes traditional sleep-temple purification rituals.
- Use the recordings as many times as you like and see if this helps you to increase the vividness and complexity of the story and scenery.
- Record your impressions of the hypnagogic journey in a notebook or dream journal; sketches and drawings are really useful, too.
- As you go about the rest of your day, try to notice if you can spot any of the journey's motifs or themes repeated in waking reality.

- You could use the hypnagogic experience as a starting point to develop narrative ideas and scenery beyond those described. Working creatively with the story will help you create a feedback system between your active imagination and the creative dreaming process.
- Read the related narrative chapter of the book a second time as a final step, just before you go to sleep at night. Allow your impressions of the story to percolate as you fall asleep, and remember your hypnagogic journey from listening to the audio recording. Try to reenact the experience. Imagine yourself back on this quest, and try to visualize your movements through the remembered space.

○ ○ ○

We can learn much from the ancient world, and in this book I wish to present to you some of the most interesting dream philosophies of antiquity. I do this with the aim of encouraging a new, modern elevation of dreaming. I would love dreaming to be recognized as a vital, divine, deeply creative, life-enhancing, and healing therapeutic practice. I would love sleep health and transcendental dreaming to be incorporated into a holistic health care system, and I believe certain dreams can really heal people.

Let us begin the initiation . . .

The Dream Initiation

Phase One
The Dawn of Dreams
Paleolithic to 10,000 BCE

The cradle rocks above an abyss, and common sense tells us that our existence is but a brief crack of light between two eternities of darkness. Although the two are identical twins, man, as a rule, views the prenatal abyss with more calm than the one he is heading for (at some forty-five hundred heartbeats an hour).

VLADIMIR NABOKOV, *SPEAK, MEMORY*

Art is undoubtedly one of the first technologies to hint at the idea of consciousness and spiritual belief. Art suggests otherworlds and souls; it illustrates future-thinking, dreams, and an afterlife. As soon as we create forms and images, we create new things to populate our dreams. In dreams, forms and images come alive and can communicate with us. By creating forms and images, we start a process, one in which our dreams can work with these creations and morph them into new versions and adaptations. With such visions carried over into the waking world and immortalized as art, the process of dream-reality feedback continues ad infinitum.

Audio track 1, "Chrysalis," is the companion to this phase.

To know where and who we are now, we must first contemplate our origins and the journey of consciousness from the remote past to the present day.

The experiences of our ancestors have formed echoic threads that extend through us today. They travel backward, through our many previous incarnations, and will journey onward, into all those yet to come. The memories of our forebears can be seen to link all of humanity. Truly, how can memory be separated from consciousness? They are spiraling twins. Consciousness happens when memories are woven together.

Some of the oldest figurative objects and cave paintings are currently dated circa 45,000 years old. Indonesian cave paintings illustrating a warty pig hunting scene,[1] and the Lion-man, or Löwenmensch, a figurine carved out of mammoth ivory found in Germany, are among these.[2] But there are certainly older examples, particularly in Australia and Africa, and excavations in 2008 at Blombos Cave in South Africa revealed what is considered to be a pigment-processing workshop.[3] A liquefied ocher mixture was produced and stored in two abalone shells a hundred thousand years ago. Ocher, bone, charcoal, grindstones, and hammerstones were part of the production tool kit. So it is reasonable to suppose that art was being created much earlier than previously thought—that it may even have been practiced to some extent by a number of early hominid species as they emerged and evolved during the Pleistocene.

The ideas that inspire art have been with all peoples, in all times. Art has been developed, exchanged, augmented, and passed down. The ability of early humans to mimic the sounds and shapes of their natural environment, to make music, song, and speech, helped enormously in the rapid transmission and evolution of ideas. Many of these early ideas are still preserved by indigenous lineages in isolated pockets all over the world. They have been maintained deep in rain forests and on mountainous islands secluded by rising seas. Art and ideas have traveled incalculable distances, journeying with our most ancient ancestors as they lived and died in relay races, using glacial highways and disappearing land bridges to traverse the globe.

THE BIRTH OF LANGUAGE AND WRITING

What is known as the Hiawatha structure, a 31-km-long geologic formation beneath the Hiawatha Glacier in Greenland, is the result of a meteoric impact thought by some scientists to have ushered in the Younger Dryas period, which reversed planetary warming and instituted planetary cooling about 12,000 to 13,000 years ago.[4] This saw the destruction of certain hot spots of established human activity and is thought to have terminated the Clovis culture, a Paleoamerican culture consisting of some of the earliest people to have lived in the Americas.

This cataclysmic impact would have caused vast wildfires locally and megafloods of surging meltwater. It would have led to increasing sea and river levels globally. The Younger Dryas was a sudden cooling period, one that saw human populations in the Northern Hemisphere migrate toward areas with more stable food sources and kinder climates. Primary sources of food had previously been the plentiful megafauna and avifauna of the fecund mammoth steppe.[5] Oh, the halcyon days of giant herbivores and cloudberries! The climatic changes during the Younger Dryas eventually sank most of what remained of this rich terrain. The mammoth steppe had straddled the northern globe, linking Eurasia and North America. Over the course of the next 1,300 years, there followed a mass extinction of megafauna such as saber-toothed cats, the giant sloth, titanis birds, and woolly mammoths. The climatic changes and new survival challenges activated by the Younger Dryas are thought to have led to the Neolithic Revolution. This was a distinct cultural shift that saw the beginnings of human settlement and agriculture in fertile river valleys, mountainous islands, and biodiverse plains. The most well-known region of this type was the Fertile Crescent, a belt of rich, arable land that arcs through Jericho and the Levant, Cyprus, Turkey (ancient Anatolia), Lebanon, Iraq, and Iran.

Many of the cultural and spiritual concepts that had been relevant and meaningful to humans before the advent of agriculture continued to evolve and develop alongside agrarian settlement and the new lifestyles required by agriculture and animal husbandry. New meanings emerged as cultures changed and adapted to their particular environments and the necessities of survival within them. Land ownership and territory as well as the protection of tribe members with both invisible boundaries and by the erection of walls, gates, and other thresholds were concepts that emerged during this time. These foundational landscaping and architectural activities delineated and circumscribed the physical and mental landscapes of early humans. These early technologies established a separation between humans and the rest of the world, and they came to define the unique regional flavors and colors of each social and spiritual system as they arose.

When it came to the invention of writing later on, the forms early societies developed were also a product of the ecology and geology of the areas they inhabited. For example, cuneiform, the distinctive wedge impressions of the writing system of the ancient Near East, was the result of an abundance of clay and reeds in the region. Its stylistic expression, therefore, is absolutely tied to its geography.

As language and writing became ever more commonplace and abstract, we might anticipate that the human mind would become more specialized. Through the innovation of language, humans became increasingly adept at dealing with abstraction, with the identification and reckoning of separate units. We became perhaps less engaged with having a direct experience of the world as a whole and more engaged with a new intellectual sphere, one that focused on valuations, possibilities, and potentials within a primarily mental world.

There can be little doubt that the idea of a soul existed among Paleolithic people. Some of the most ancient burials suggest the idea of the continuation of the soul beyond physical death. Early nomadic groups emerging in the Levant during the Upper Paleolithic, in particular the Aurignacian, Ahmarian, and later the Natufian cultures, offer some of the earliest examples of ritual burial and funerary rites. The concepts of soul and afterlife were probably drawn from lived experience. Perhaps pre-language, the human mind was primed for a more flexible perception of the world around it. Without a name for all things, experience of the world was likely more kinesthetic, synesthetic, plastic, and association-based and less defined by the boundaries of ego and self-identification. Dreams are chiefly generated and driven by imagery, language, and association. So perhaps the world of our ancestors was more dreamlike for them than it is for us today. I propose that an ancient predisposition toward a dreamlike perception of the world, and especially a less robust identification with self, would have resulted in more out-of-body episodes and other lucid-type dream phenomena.

GAMES, WORDS, DIVINATION, AND DREAMING

Games, language, divination, and dreams are inextricable elements of our cultural history and have greatly contributed to the type of consciousness we have today. All sorts of animals play and dream, but the intricacies of human games and dreams, made possible by our unique physiology and vocal capabilities, have elevated both the game and the dream to extraordinary levels. The very nature of most games necessitates anticipating and predicting the future and calculating likely outcomes. Likewise, dreams prepare organisms for future events by allowing a kind of pre-experience of them, and as such they are thought to have an evolutionary function.[6] And like dreaming, game-playing is also entangled with language; it may even be the foundation on which language developed, as developments in divination and game-playing would have been further encouraged by increasing linguistic acuity. Our dream experiences would have been significantly altered by these new avenues of consciousness, and this represents a distinction from the consciousness of other members of the animal kingdom.

When we play games we are inventing. Invention generates habits; habits, over time, restructure our brain connectivity; and this in turn influences the way we see our world. Throughout our lifetime, neural plasticity enables the physical structures in our brain and body to reorganize.[7] This promotes growth and connectivity in well-exercised areas of the brain, and it prunes back and shrinks to economize energy in other less-well-exercised areas. It does all this in response to our environment, activities, habits, physicality, experiences, and encounters. In this way we truly have a symbiotic relationship with the world around us. To a great extent it could be said that we curate our reality in response to an ongoing dialogue between the inside and outside world.

As can still be seen in the world today, the way in which people relate to the world and to other people is subject to extraordinary variability.

THE DEVELOPMENT OF STAR KNOWLEDGE

For most of human history, the night sky remained undimmed by the light pollution ushered in by the electrical age. It is not hard to appreciate why our ancestors were so entranced and mesmerized by brilliant stellar vistas. We know ancient people recognized patterns and observed the cyclical dance of the planets. They would have witnessed celestial influences during meteor showers and comet passes. They would have wondered at solar and lunar eclipses, and they would have paid attention to every other sort of space and weather phenomenon. They felt themselves to be subject to the motion of the stars—which is why the personification of stars and planets became the earliest divine entities. The stars emphasized human anchorage to Earth and helped humans anticipate the flux of seasons and the alternating effects of moving celestial bodies.

Stars were the first language we learned to "read," and in many ways they were perceived as precognizant of the future. Perhaps ancient observers spoke of their extraordinary distance and vastness, their immortality and omnipotence. It would have been noted from our perspective on Earth that the stars stayed mostly constantly shining throughout countless generations. For early peoples, the stars marked time and passage. They hinted at a divine and eternal omnipresence.

We know from written accounts that early watchers of the skies in the ancient Near East recorded particular events occurring on Earth during specific celestial phenomena, such that the next time the same celestial event occurred it was supposed that similar terrestrial events would occur again. Phenomena frequently did match up in terms of the seasonal celestial calendar for hunting and gathering because these astronomical practices were likely derived from older, preliterate star lore. This kind of thinking turned into the prophetic art of celestial omens,[8] which were applied to the lives of individuals and communities to become the formal merged arts and sciences of astrology and astronomy.

By observing the heavens, ancient peoples were able to develop a sense of time and place for themselves on Earth. This terrestrial time ran concurrent with the much greater, infinitely expansive divine time that belonged to the immortals. In this way ancient humans could make predictions about the future by closely observing their relationship to the divine time of the immortals above.

To better chart the stars and learn their language, our ancestors made maps of those stars that were visible in the night sky by creating arrangements of standing stones. They encoded what they saw in the nighttime sky as paintings on cave walls; they etched them into pots, tattooed them on their bodies, and carved them on rock faces. They watched the stars sparkle in bodies of water. In this way, perhaps, they could see them as reflections of heavenly fish swimming in an infinite and mysterious dark ocean. The reflective surfaces of pools, lakes, ponds, and puddles opened them to the possibility of another dimension, and the mirage of eternity on Earth was revealed. The stars dwell in an imperishable realm, completely beyond the mortal reach of humans. Perhaps this is evidence of an ancient yearning to draw the immortals down to Earth, to forge a bond with them and receive their blessings for their own immortality. This is echoed in many of the early creation myths, where the personified Heaven and Earth copulate to produce gods and mortals.

With all of this kind of mental activity, our ancestors invited ritual and magic into the world, and rituals and magical thinking still make up a significant part of modern life.

Magic always begins at nighttime, when the reality of our position in space is revealed, when we enter into the realm of dreams . . .

DREAMS OF THE ANCIENTS

The ancient preoccupation with knowing the future was surely encouraged by dreamed experiences, which are often full of future intimations. The earliest forms of prophecy are recorded in the accounts of dreams. It is likely, I believe, that the deepening complexity of our thought-worlds in dreams and other altered states inspired the earliest ideas about spiritual reality, the soul, the afterlife, and, ultimately, religion.

Dreams have a vaporous nature, and prior to written accounts, which have so far exclusively been found only among the artifacts of literate, elite, more advanced civilizations, we have no definitive evidence about the dreams of ordinary people in the very distant past, though it is possible that some cave paintings were an attempt to illustrate the dreams of the ordinary people who recorded them. From my own dream experiences I can identify dreamlike images in much prehistoric art, for instance, the oftentimes disproportionate scale of insects, birds and animals in comparison with humans, is something that occurs in dreams. In dreams attention seems to increase the size of an entity to facilitate closer examination of it. I often find that in my dreams, insects, birds, and other animals are much larger than they appear in real life; in particular small birds appear as toddler-size. Dreamlike auras of light often appear around the heads of humanoid figures, and characters frequently morph in and out of a variety of human and animal forms. When I look at ancient art, I sense an expression of the altered states of hypnagogic trance, dreams, and sleep. In dreams we often find that scale is a matter of our own focus. As a philosophical experiment, we can only attempt to intuit what kind of dream life preliterate people may have had. We can use our imagination to contextualize dream phenomenon based on what we know about the conditions of the time period and through observing our own dreams closely. We can contemplate and assess other material evidence that has been left behind. We can observe the major themes of dream culture that developed later on in history, and we can explore the dream beliefs of the world's oldest cultures that have survived into the modern era, such as those of the people of the First Nations of Australia. And we can be as sensitive as possible to any other clues that hint at the way ancient people perceived their inner and outer worlds.

MAGICAL PRACTICES

Sympathetic magic is a term used by ethnographers, anthropologists, historians, and practitioners of magic to describe the assumption that a person (or thing) can be supernaturally affected by actions directed toward something that represents them. The term was first coined more than a hundred years ago by James George Frazer in his book *The Golden Bough*. Frazer identified two elements of sympathetic magic, which essentially expresses the idea of like begetting like through the law of similarity or the law of contagion. With the law of similarity is the idea that similar things possess a kinship and connected power. For example, a fruit or herb that resembles a particular body part, for instance the similarity of a walnut to a human brain, can improve the health of that organ in humans. The law of contagion is the idea that when two, usually animate, objects come into contact with one another, they can exchange qualities, properties, and power.

Sympathetic magic was probably the earliest manifestation of magical practice and spiritual belief. Some scholars make a case for cave paintings being such a form, particularly those of successful hunting scenes.[9] If so, cave paintings may be an attempt by early peoples to cast positive influence into the future by rendering on the cave wall a desired outcome for themselves and their community.

The term *sympathetic magic* can also be applied to the alchemical law of correspondence, which in alchemy states that the essence or power of a thing can be transferred or imbued by coming into contact with it. This can be achieved by binding or by ingestion, absorption, ritual touch, burning, sacrifice, name-giving, blood-letting, and immersion.

Sympathetic magic has been incorporated into all of the modern religions that developed out of the ancient nature religions of antiquity. Baptism, christening, Mass, offerings, pilgrimage, and sacrifice, for example, are still some of the most important magical rites of a modern religious person's pious, righteous, and definitely not pagan life.

In ancient Egypt and the Near East, magic was very much intertwined with writing and language,[10] which has a profound relationship with dream content. Our dreaming mind processes language and words differently from our waking mind.[11] In dreams we often express intellectual concepts or ideas with images, symbols, and scenes. We employ puns, wordplay, and association. For example, we might dream of someone we haven't seen or had any special interest in for years, but we may often find that the clue to the dream lies in the person's name. For example after an injury to your leg you might dream of your old neighbor Tony (toe, knee). Or after reading the *Glass Bead Game* by Hermann Hesse and musing on the Buddhist concept of the illusory nature of reality, you might dream of someone you knew at school called Maya. This is classic dream association. The sound values of words are vital components of thorough dream interpretation.

RITUALS FOR THE DEAD

A case can be made for the existence of widely dispersed prehistoric and pre-language dream cultures. Ancient ideas about the reality of dreaming most likely centered on contacting ancestors and supernatural beings and included the idea of an underworld or celestial realm where one could visit these disembodied spirits. This idea is beautifully preserved by Australia's First Nations peoples in what they call the Dreaming, or *Alcheringa*. The Dreaming is a creative consciousness continuum, perpetuated over millennia.[12] The concept is impossible to render in English, as it is a lived experience of the world and its spirits. It is something like an active, living story of the world, where all life is connected and preserved in an eternal memory. The world *is* the story, a spiritual reality, constantly evolving and coalescing into matter. The idea is that in dreaming, the dreamer is able to remember the beginnings of the world and can take an active role in its continuing creative processes.

Undoubtedly one of the most striking and recognizable features of dreams is that they allow us to intimately interact with the deceased. This may have been the first phenomenon of consciousness, the first liminal experience that pointed our ancient ancestors toward the idea of an afterlife and in particular suggested the idea of an immortal spirit form and an otherworld.

We shall have to use our imaginations somewhat here, as pre-writing societies had no means of explicitly communicating these concepts other than through art, symbols, and rituals. As is evident historically, a good deal of wildly speculative interpretation can be made through these mediums. To a great extent, and often unknowingly, contemporary investigators cannot help but view such symbols and imagery through the lens and filter of modernity. We of course cannot assume that ancient people recognized biological death in the same way we do today. Likewise, we cannot expect that ancient people saw dream experiences, psychedelic reveries, or other liminal states as mind-generated, imaginal phenomenon, as has been the trend for the past century. I believe intimations of the earliest dream cultures reside in our first death cultures.

Complex rituals in response to bodily death are some of the earliest signs of human culture, significantly predating the development of agriculture. Objects of value were frequently buried with the dead. Often it seems burial items appear to have been ceremonially broken, as though they were tainted by death's aura, and also perhaps reserving them symbolically for use by the deceased. Or perhaps it suggests that these objects were viewed as living, that they should cease to be alongside their owner. Some items reflect the idea of sympathetic magic, such as a powerful animal's body part carefully buried with an injured corresponding part of a human.[13] Burials containing objects of power and status might suggest a provision for another world and another animation. Sites of internment appear to become places for ancestor connection, places to congregate, feast, and perhaps sleep. Dreams in which the living meet with the dead surely inspired ideas about an otherworld, about a spirit realm in which the dead live on.

Initiatic Story: Chrysalis

Mendi closed her eyes. She conjured an image of the aurochs. Her fingertips were wet and shining with gritty ocher. She felt for the rough rock and drew a wide line, arcing up toward the tail end of the beast. She felt the creature's vital spine rise through her own bones as she gave it new life on stone. Pleased with her first stroke and with her eyes wide open now, she worked in the steady, smokeless light of her sandstone lamp.

A puddle of liquid fat at the pebble's center glittered in the darkness. The aurochs danced before her as a phantom, and she traced his shapes as he moved.

Drawing the thick neck of the beast next, his head and then his fine, forward-curving sacred horns, she felt the satisfyingly smooth texture of horn pass through her left palm. Using both her hands, she dipped her fingers into the damp mixture of ocher and ash. She marked the deep creases of the animal's heavy chest and filled out his dark, curled coat. She delineated the robust legs, a little shorter at the front, and she flicked down the delicate line of his long, tasseled and bedraggled tail.

The aurochs came alive on the surface of the cave wall, animated by lamplight rippling across the uneven stone. A shimmering rush of tiny quartz flecks around the image imparted an aura of magic and creation. Mendi had a sense of the spirit of this beast. This was a generative act . . . Mendi created the future . . .

She made the signs of her people, the simple symbols of place and time. The sign for her name: mountain. Now the aurochs was fixed in this world, anchored to Mendi. She felt a mysterious, unreachable new reality. This reality seemed to pool at the ethereal edge of the world she existed in now . . .

Mendi wondered about the flying sorcerers, the butterflies. Her people called them *sorgin*. As a child she had watched them studiously, those dull-colored caterpillars. She had observed them monotonously chewing bright green leaves, their eyes dull and unblinking as though they were in a trance. These worms ate until they were too swollen to move. When they became thoroughly stiffened by their sated hunger and newly acquired mass, they dangled, corpselike, from branches. Their bodies suspended by a single thread, they encased themselves in a rigid, papery shell. Mendi loved to watch these pupae dangling in the wind. She breathed on them. She held them in her warm palm. She lifted them up to the sun and looked closely for ripples of movement. She hoped for chinks of transparency. Best of all, though, was when they finally broke open . . . When they opened, completely new beings emerged. These new beings unrolled damp, delicate wings. The most beautiful flying creatures they were. They almost immediately took to wing, to the air, without any hesitation. It was as if they had always known their future. Some had painted eyes and some the most amazing rainbow colors . . . They were pure sorcery . . .

As a child, Mendi ate one of these alchemical capsules. She wanted to ingest its transformative magic, assume its power. In this cold cave she now remembered the texture of the chrysalis shell against her childish teeth. On her tongue she could still taste the bitter liquid body of the sorcerer. It was her first magical rite, the first sacrament, and this primitive caterpillar was the first Christ.

This was how she imagined herself now, enclosed within a cocoon. Slowing her heart and breathing with the throbs of the flame from her lamp, Mendi felt the power of that ancient pill finally working. In this moment she knew that it had always been working, and she had a sense of the future. Through half-closed eyes, she watched her aurochs, the ocher still glistening with moisture. Mendi lay against the earth . . . feeling the coolness of the Maker's body against her own. Her skin was infused with the Maker's fertile essence, her heart slowed. She felt for the Maker's pulse.

The lamp burned up the last dregs of fat, and it suddenly went out. Darkness. The glowing afterimage of the lamp's flame echoed in her eyes . . . the smell of smoke . . . cold flames hovering pink and green in the rich, black air of the cave. The impression lingered in her gaze, following the movements of her pupils as she searched for the aurochs.

Other senses crowded in . . . Now she felt the distant soft dripping of the spring. She lay very still, expanding her awareness of the blood and breath moving through her body. She felt the rumble of distant water beneath her. She listened to the opening and closing of tiny organisms, a popping sound, like mussels and limpets in a rock pool starved of water. Fungal threads were stretching and shrinking, channeling nutrients to new extremities, creeping their intelligent lacework through guano-patterned, light-starved stone. Solitary, mineral-rich drops were falling from the cave ceiling to the floor. Mendi heard the scrabbling of a young bat reverberate along a tunnel that led deeper into the earth.

She saw thousands of open eyes in the darkness and watched them blink. The sound of their blinking meshed with the stretching of growing molds and the pings of cave spiders plucking their webs. Slowly these eyes transformed into a magnificent, moonless night sky. The firmament swarmed with luminous souls and swirled with radiant, ancient life.

A timeless entirety reached down for Mendi now. She knew the heavens sent orbs of light to the Earth; she had seen this.

Such blinding power. The stars that fell from the sky made great walls of white light. This was a light that could rip through forests, that exploded sap-saturated trees and evaporated lakes. This light scorched the earth and made crystals from frenzied fusions of space rock and sand. Mendi had found such crystals with her people, when they went stalking the aurochs in the vast, deep earth bowl. This bowl had been scoured out by a star a long time ago. Mendi had only seen the smallest of fallen stars herself . . .

There were many stories of world-shattering stars . . . falling stars that boiled rivers, blackened the sky, and swallowed up so much life. The earth in this bowl had healed, covered now with green, but the depression of the star's impact remained. Mendi had found some crystals around the crater. They were prickled, like newborn hedgehogs. They were the color of murky pond water. A little sunlight filtered through them. She had collected many of these crystals from the sky.

She now vividly relived this scene from her life, seeing it play out in all its fine detail, inside the mind of the cave. She couldn't tell whether her eyes were open or closed, the blackness of the cave all-consuming. Her body had no boundaries, her human form was bonded to the Maker. Her imaginings and feelings were filling the dark space with color and sound. She suddenly saw the glassy hedgehog stones. They began to squirm in her dream fingers, their gummy, blind eyes opening. She saw a star fall, and she felt herself being dragged upward in the air, held by a vortex of light and shadow . . .

The world changed and morphed around her body. Now she rose through a hole in the cave. She entered a circle of blue light, and mingling with fast-moving clouds, she felt their wispy coolness. She saw herself flying alongside a great eagle, sharing the feeling of the eagle's beak and claws. She knew the readiness of avian eyes.

Seeing through eagle eyes, she noticed the shivering fur of a gray hare. She watched it darting through long, dry grass very far below. It was so far away . . . the vision was astounding. She knew how it is to see like an eagle. She felt the skin of the hare, held tightly around its legs.

She felt the soft pads of its energetic paws and the friction of its claws. As the hare, she scrabbled against the chalky gravel underfoot. But as the eagle, she plummeted down, falling through the sky, as swift as a spear, plunging into the hare's panicked heart.

Eagle Mendi felt a throb of life pulse through her honeycombed bones. She tasted the hot, sweet, metallic, living blood of a quick and righteous death. The weight of the large hare in her claws weighed on her wings. She took the heavy, limp body back to her nest . . .

The nest was filled with pond-water hoglets. It was lined with oakmoss and the oily feathers of previous kills. The hedgehog babies clamored for her breast. They stretched their toothless mouths wide and wrinkled their blind, pink eyes and snouts against the bright light.

Again the walls turned into eyes. The earth had eyes and ears and a heartbeat. Mendi knew herself to be lying in the belly of the Maker. She felt neither dead nor alive. Instead, she was suspended somewhere between this world and another. The face of the aurochs flashed alive and swooped in front of her head. She was at the bottom of a crystal lake now, and the agentle beast's face dipped into the cold, limpid water above her . . .

She saw every detail . . . the most precise and perfect vision. With the eyes of an eagle, she saw tiny hairs strung with mirrored bubbles. She saw wet, sad eyes and flaring nostrils. Proud horns sliced through the water. Now she was taken away again, finding herself holding an aurochs's horn at a burial, weighing it in her right hand. She felt the horn scratch against a string of fox teeth, teeth carved with the signs of her people. She felt the carving of her own sign with her thumb. She gently draped the necklace of fox teeth over the middle of a small, still body in a hole. Its knees were drawn up to its chest, its arms tucked in . . . It was a woman. Was it Mendi? She placed the horn close to the dead woman's head. She blinked—and she was back in the cave.

Like the sorgin now, Mendi crawled into the light. She emerged into the blinding sun, her wings yet to unfold. She was deprived of flight in this life . . .

Phase Two
Into the Bronze Age
Neolithic, Chalcolithic, Bronze Age
10,000 to 4500 BCE

At night no sweet dream overtakes me on my bed and no favor is manifest to me. But now, my [god], harness together your strength and that of the Protective-deity. I never even inquired through a seeress whether you, my god, ordained an illness for me from the womb (lit. inside) of my mother.

FROM THE HITTITE PRAYER OF
KANTUZZILI, TRANSLATED BY ITAMAR SINGER

It seems entirely plausible that the practice of dream incubation would have become ritualized very early on, perhaps evolving out of a combination of meaningful ancestral rites such as communal sleeping at gravesides, the commonplace but numinous qualities of ordinary dream experience, and the emergence of certain supernatural dream motifs and archetypes. One such archetype is that of the divine feminine.

Women are guardians of life; they have the fantastic power to be able to bring entirely new people into the world. In earlier times, this

---

Audio track 2, "The Head," is the companion to this phase.

was a gift fraught with tremendous danger and risk, of course, as many women died in childbirth, making infant mortality rates considerably higher than they are today. It is maybe logical then that our ancient ancestors anticipated a feminine involvement at the other end of life, a female as the natural sentinel or gatekeeper of death. Let us consider the possibility that ancient people believed death to be a rebirthing into another space-time—a theme that persists in subsequent afterlife myths. The archetype of the Great Ancestress appeared long before the Bronze Age and was one of the first arguably *divine* images valued by ancient people. She functioned as a portal, linking the world of the living to the world of the dead. She refracted in the mirror-mind of the ancient imagination, perhaps somewhat like the divine twin trope that appears in later mythology, in which twins represent the dual divine and mortal aspects of humanity. Often seen as the children of the sky gods, the divine twins functioned as healers and protectors of humanity. The ancient female death guide, as a mother archetype, expressed the fullness of feminine power resolved only by death. Dreams would be the natural place to meet this Great Ancestress. In this subzone, her role mirrored, she could act as psychopomp, delivering the dying to the world of the dead.

At the end of our lives, the Great Ancestress can show us the way to death. She can help us relinquish our final breath, just as she pushed us toward taking our first inward gasp at the very moment we entered into being.

GODDESSES AS PERSONIFICATIONS OF NATURAL FORCES

The female icons explored in this chapter were often of an astral nature, the personifications of stars or planets. Terrestrial goddesses could also be personified mountains, trees, bodies of water, and caves. As we have seen in the previous chapter, the stars were considered omnipotent and precognizant of the future. This future was disclosed through the arrangement of stars in the night sky and was readable by early humans who were star literate. Star literacy is the wholly expanded, conscious perception of the world and the galaxy. It is an impressive, cosmos-connecting skill set, one that demands admiration and respect, which many indigenous people as well as professional and amateur astronomers and astrologers still possess.

The Great Ancestress was sometimes regarded as the Creatrix of the universe. As a woman is uniquely able to give birth to new human offspring, she would seem the obvious candidate to be the mother of the universe. The dreams sought by her supplicants may have offered oracular insight, divine intervention, wise counsel, spontaneous healing, contact with the ancestors, and perhaps even miracle-working, likely with a special emphasis on trouble-free childbirth. Desired dream outcomes like this were common themes among experienced dreamers and in the increasingly prescriptive dream-incubating technologies that were recorded later in the ancient Near East, Egypt, and Greece.

Culture, convention, and the material world directly influence dreaming, providing context and creating content. We know that dreaming is culturally specific and is therefore deeply informed by prevailing concepts of reality, self, and other. So to understand the dream lives of our ancient ancestors, we must attempt to evoke their worldviews.

THE GREAT ANCESTRESS

Many of the earliest identifiable dream-delivering entities in Anatolia and the Near East were female deities associated with the overworld of Heaven, the realm of the gods and an underworld where the dead were thought to reside alongside chthonic divinities. The Great Ancestress seems to give birth in the heavens, and later she draws one's soul down into the heart of the earth, perhaps to begin the cycle of life once again.

Many female figurines certainly appear to have once been venerated artifacts. By creating a personification of something that is otherwise too vast and intangible to comprehend, an artisan could contain the essence of a subject within a representation, and this made it possible to comprehend and worship an otherwise ineffable concept. The creator of an icon could craft a sort of psychic target at which one's adoration and attention could be directed, projected; and perhaps even in the many minds of our ancestors these objects could store the psychic energy directed at them. There continues to be an understanding throughout the ancient Near East, Egypt, and Greece that statues could contain the essence of a divine being. Statues would be ritually anointed, dressed, and taken on processions. Often their placement in ritual sites was seen to activate and transform space into a holy precinct.

There is a clear continuity of culturally significant female icons that persists throughout the earliest human cultures. Their presence seems to be intrinsic to whatever spiritual ideas these people had as well as to the formation of their blossoming philosophies. I believe a basic concept of the Great Ancestress developed in the Chalcolithic and Bronze Age periods, growing organically out of a prehistoric vision of the world as a life-giving female entity. This essential premise evolved naturally in response to the terrific array of conditions and aesthetic factors that human settlers recalibrated to once they settled in new terrains. Notably, as we have previously considered, these conditions might have included orientation to and visibility of celestial objects, weather, duration of days and nights, geology, and local flora and fauna.

GÖBEKLI TEPE

Göbekli Tepe is an extraordinary and enigmatic Neolithic archaeological site near the city of Şanlıurfa, in southeastern Turkey. Its existence was first recorded in a university survey in 1963, but the excavations instigated in 1995 by German archaeologist Klaus Schmidt confirmed his suspicions that the site had incredibly important cultural significance. Schmidt continued working on the project until his death in 2014, and his fantastic discoveries required historians to rewrite time lines, which transformed the archaeological record considerably. Schmidt believed Göbekli Tepe to be the world's earliest temple and found no sign of human habitation or settlement; however, newer findings have updated some of his suppositions.

Continuing excavations led by supervising archaeologist Lee Clare have more recently revealed evidence of human settlement at the site, but even now less than 5 percent of Göbekli Tepe has been excavated.[1] Its true antiquity is therefore hard to pinpoint precisely; however, it is currently dated to between circa 9500 and 8000 BCE—about 12,000 years old. The structures uncovered at Göbekli Tepe demonstrate that even in this very ancient time period there existed a certain type of settled, organized village life, with features such as division of labor, large-scale architectural and artistic projects, and the management and distribution of collective resources. These are some of the social characteristics and innovations that once had been thought to have emerged only with the development of agriculture, which previously was believed to have made its first appearance in the Mesopotamian region. The semi-sedentary habits of the ancient residents of Göbekli Tepe are similar to those seen in the Natufian culture of the Levant, a Late Epipaleolithic society that emerged about 15,000 years ago in modern-day Syria, Israel, Palestine, and Jordan.[2] The Natufians were protoagriculturists and cooperative villagers who had a range of ritual practices that reflected a complex set of beliefs, most notably around death. They developed agriculture in response to a scarcity of resources and desertification of their homeland, the result of climatic changes during the Younger Dryas—the planetary cooling period that occurred roughly between 12,900 and 11,600 years ago.

The most distinctive features of Göbekli Tepe are its megalithic T-shaped limestone pillars, carved with obsidian and bone tools. These towering stones are decorated mostly with anthropomorphic and zoomorphic forms. The pillars are arranged in circles, creating a number of individual enclosures. Many of these enclosures are thought to have been backfilled purposely by their builders, suggesting to many that the arrangement of stones were orientated to align with particular planets and stars. This discovery has led some, such as theoretical physicist and chemical engineer Martin Sweatman and prehistoric art specialist and researcher Alistair Coombs, to conclude that the circles represent celestial timekeeping devices, much like England's Stonehenge,[3] by which heavenly movements could be accurately measured to correspond with the seasonal cycles of Earth.[4] The life cycles of plants and animals, their seasonally dictated abundance as well as their dry spells, clearly occur according to cyclical cosmic rhythms. These rhythms can be best anticipated by observing, recording, and remembering astral arrangements.

The brilliant astronomical knowledge of Australia's First Nations peoples as well as that of many long-surviving tribal societies across Africa are extraordinary examples of the preservation of astral wisdom, which can be traced all the way back to the Stone Age.[5] This suggests the possibility that star lore was already known to the wave of human migrants who traveled out of Africa and across Southeast Asia to Australia some 72,000 years ago.[6] That this knowledge was not taken with earlier and later waves of Africa's modern human population and dispersed elsewhere seems highly unlikely. Genetic studies show that the earliest of these population movements began about 220,000 years ago.[7]

Continuing art and oral storytelling traditions use recognized symbolism and mythic language to communicate information about the intimate, localized relationships between the heavens and life on Earth. These primitive technologies helped to encode essential environmental information into landworks that could function as almanacs. This celestial plotting on Earth enabled the earliest peoples of Africa and Australia to track important patterns in nature—for example, when animals mated or laid eggs, plants blossomed, or fish ran. The stars, therefore, transmitted undeniably vital information, facilitating human survival and success. It is notable that these cultures, the oldest and most consistently maintained on Earth, did not develop classical scripts or alphabets, yet their stories have been successfully transmitted through time. These ancient stories and symbols have helped preserve a precious window through which we can observe how the ancients viewed their world. To give an example of just how vast and all-encompassing this knowledge can be, Australian anthropologist Charles Mountford, in his 1976 book *Nomads of the Australian Desert,* wrote the following: "The Aborigines of the desert are aware of every star in their firmament, down to the fourth magnitude, and most, if not all, of these stars would have myths associated with them."[8]

Similarly, the Göbekli Tepe circles may have served to record dates based on the precession of the equinoxes, with animal symbols representing ancient constellations. There is even the suggestion that some features of Göbekli Tepe may memorialize and warn of a disastrous encounter with the Taurid meteor stream, which occurred during the Younger Dryas. Specifically, the so-called Vulture Stone, or Pillar 43, is believed to be a symbolic stela inscribed with this information.[9] Noteworthy is the fact that most of the carvings represent animals in fierce attack modes as well as poisonous or dangerous beasts—snakes, scorpions, boars, lions, and so on. This has led some scholars to believe that parts of the site served some sort of initiatory or training function and were designed to induce feelings of threat and fear to prepare initiates for danger,[10] though it is worth considering that if the constellations were represented as animal forms then that threat may have been expected to come from the sky.

Among the smaller finds at Göbekli Tepe, besides totemic animal carvings, there are a number of figures that feature human phallic and vulval iconography and certain images and engravings that suggest a composite of both female and male genitalia.[11] There has been a tendency to categorize phallic, vulval, and voluptuous images created by our ancient ancestors as "fertility figures." Considering the sophistication of the symbolic languages that were clearly being employed even in those early times, to call these images fertility figures doesn't reveal anything about the true nature of these objects. Our ancient ancestors evidently possessed a complex tool kit of symbols for succinct expression. These figures likely have a whole range of specific meanings that are inextricable from the context of their particular location, space, and time. For example, some may have acted as markers or charms in earthworks that functioned as celestial maps. They could have pinpointed exact moments on these calendars for harvesting, animal migrations, ceremonial events, and planting. Some may have been part of domestic or communal shrines adoring the all-providing Mother Vulva and fertilizing Phallus. They may have been designed for healing and magic, for evoking harmony and balance. Some may simply be Neolithic erotica, but in this case could the energizing and vitalizing force of sexual potency be the grandmother of religious fervor?

If, as in the Australian Aboriginal Dreaming, the things of the world are a living language of creation, then by using images that recall the things of the world, it is possible to write a story. And such a story, written on the *prima materia* of the world, becomes part of the alchemical tapestry of life.

ÇATALHÖYÜK

One of Anatolia's most beautifully preserved archaeological treasures is the Neolithic and Chalcolithic proto-city settlement of Çatalhöyük, located 338 miles from Göbekli Tepe. In its jostling clusters of honeycombed and highly decorated dwellings that housed thousands of people at its peak, we can see a clear thematic recurrence of the enigmatic iconography used at Göbekli Tepe. Catalhöyük provides greater context for the imagery. The arrangement and design of this settlement and its individual though interconnected cells is a wonderful illustration of the early psychosocial and ecosocial adaptations made by humans in human-built environments[12]—an emerging interrelation of corpus and domus, the body and the home. The design of a home reflects the perceived parameters of the body and becomes a microcosm of the outer world and a macrocosm of the self. In this mini universe, human intervention creates order and meaning, an architectural axis mundi that defines place and home for any given person in human society. Within the home we exist in this familiar point on the terrestrial surface, intersected by the four cardinal directions, between Heaven and Earth.

Before human settlement, when we wandered the Earth as nomads, our sense of place was a continually reorganizing, evolving, living process, a perpetually updated covenant between our body, Earth, and the stars. When we travel in modern times we are mostly thinking of the starting point, the route, and an ultimate destination or return. What would it have been like to wander into the truly unknown?

The famous Seated Woman of Çatalhöyük is a clay figurine of a formidable naked giantess seated on a throne. Her hands rest on the heads of big felines, possibly leopards. Her huge belly and breasts suggest pregnancy, and she may also be in the process of giving birth. This association of the feminine with feline creatures and the throne is a central theme of a common motif in ancient art of the Near East and Mediterranean, the Potnia Theron, or Mistress of Animals, of which this seated woman is considered to be one of the earliest examples. We will explore the Potnia Theron image in the context of domestication later on. But the image of the throne also filters through into the conception of the much later Egyptian goddess Auset, or Isis, whose ancient Egyptian name means "throne." The original throne is the primeval mound or mountain, the first eruption of divine creation out of chaos, the protuberance of terrestrial life that became the seat of the Creatrix goddess.

There appears to have been gender equality in Çatalhöyük society. Men and women enjoyed the same resources but also suffered the same hardships. Members of the female population died earlier than those of the male population due to childbirth and the many injuries sustained from an equal division of hard labor. They ate the same diet and had similarly meaningful burials. Certain members of society, of any sex, seem to have been revered, and these people received special burials with more elaborate grave goods. The deceased were buried in the homes of the living, reiterating the idea of the home as axis mundi, transforming the repeatedly lime-plastered floors of these structures into private underworlds. Headless bodies have also been found, as well as burials with extraneous skulls. Orientation of graves and positioning of burials within the home appear to conform to a complex set of rules dictated by age, status, and even the transitional state of the domicile.[13] Like some of their Levantine contemporaries, the people of Çatalhöyük occasionally took the heads of the dead with them when they moved, providing evidence for the existence of a skull cult.[14]

The skulls of aurochs and bulls (*bucrania*) are the most frequent artistic motif used in Çatalhöyük and may be an early indication of the adoration of a thunder sky god associated with beneficent rainfall. Other images frequently used include wildly voluptuous female figures, leopards, and bears. The precise religious significance of these symbols appears to be recorded in later ritual texts of the indigenous Hatti culture, a

Bronze Age people who inhabited Central Anatolia. Hatti cosmology demonstrates a continuation of the religious iconography of Çatalhöyük, ritual centers such as Göbekli Tepe, and other settlements in the region. The Earth goddess of the Hatti gives birth to the bull, god of thunder and rainfall, while the leopard is the Hatti goddess of the sun.

Among the highly decorated wall reliefs, symbols, and paintings that are found in every home in Çatalhöyük, there are also many images of vultures clasping skulls in the their talons and flying into the sky. There has been the suggestion that dead bodies may have been intentionally de-fleshed by vulture excarnation before interment.[15] The bodies of important persons are also thought to have had secondary burials. De-fleshing by carrion birds is not an uncommon practice elsewhere. Sky burials have long been practiced in parts of China, Tibet, Nepal, Persia, India, and Mongolia, persisting into the present day. The possibility of vulture excarnation in Çatalhöyük would, however, make the site one of the oldest in the world to employ this practice. Here, a dead body could be left out on a rooftop, maybe of some designated charnel house, to avoid predation from scavenging land animals. The houses of Çatalhöyük were all clustered together with access via the roofs. Vulture excarnation is minimally destructive; it usually leaves ligaments and tendons intact and thus enables an otherwise picked-cleaned skeleton to remain anatomically connected. The result is a perfectly prepared corpse for intramural burial, where of course putrefaction would have been a very unpleasant problem. Putrefaction was also likely to have been considered spiritually impure and thus involved certain restrictions and taboos.

There is evidence that the sleeping platforms of these dwellings were intentionally positioned over the embedded graves of the deceased.[16] This makes a strong case for the idea that these ancient people of Anatolia wanted to be close to their ancestors during sleep and may have been purposefully dreaming with the dead. In dreams, perhaps these ancient people felt they were able to keep a continuity of consciousness, a space for their ancestors and other family members to have ongoing agency in their lives. This might also explain the habit of taking skulls with them when they moved.

OLD WOMAN RITUALS

The Hittites were an ancient group of Indo-European people, Iron Age pioneers, domesticators of horses, and a highly mobile military empire. They moved into Asia Minor and established themselves in Central Anatolia and took control of the territory of the Hatti people about 2000 BCE. They developed a reputation as "god collectors" and are known to have absorbed many of the gods of surrounding regions. In particular they fully incorporated the pantheon and worldview of the indigenous people of the Land of Hatti, a name the Hittites retained and which became known in their time as "The Land of 1,000 Gods," due to their god hoarding. The Hatti of Bronze Age Central Anatolia are known to have worshipped Earth as a female form. In Hatti/Hittite mythology the Great Mother Goddess Hannahanna gave birth to the storm god Taru, who was represented by a bull or an aurochs. Their sun goddess was Furušemu (or Wurunšemu), in Hittite times identified as the Sun Goddess of Arinna. The sun goddess was often represented as a leopard. Here we see not only a relationship with the art of Çatalhöyük but also undeniable parallels with the early mythology of Crete, where there was also a solar goddess cult, ever-present bucranial motifs, and even bull-leaping rituals of great importance.

In ancient Hatti there existed a well-documented and long-lived culture of divination and oracle reading, invariably performed by especially gifted and trained women.[17] These specialist soothsayers were known as the Old Women, and their rituals were called Old Woman rituals. When important members of society wanted to know their future, desired to break an enchantment, or were undecided about the best course of action to take, they would undoubtedly consult an Old Woman. The Old Woman had the power to call in favors from the goddesses and gods, so those in need of divine intervention would seek the word of the Old Woman.

These traditions survived into the Iron Age Indo-European Hittite culture, which subsumed the indigenous population of Hatti and established its own patriarchal, military-orientated society. Many of

Hatti's spiritual beliefs and their numerous gods and goddesses were maintained by the new rulers, and the Old Woman rituals continued to be recorded in the predominate Indo-European languages of Hittite, Luwian, Lycian, Palaic, and Carian. Some texts were recorded in the native language of Hattic, in Hurrian, the Hurro-Urartian language of northern Mesopotamia's Mitanni Kingdom, and on occasion in Akkadian, which was adopted by the Hittite scribes for diplomatic communiqués. Despite their patriarchal bent, the military-minded newcomers apparently could not shake off the sorcery of the Old Woman, as her prophetic skills were far too valuable. These women therefore retained a very privileged position at court.

It is attested that the Old Women came from all over Anatolia, suggesting that their craft already had great antiquity. There was likely some sort of formal training and a canonical tradition within the culture, as the ritual and incantatory texts have considerable consistency over a vast period of time and geographical range. Diviners and ritual practitioners of significant importance and prestige, they would be called in to resolve everything from domestic squabbles to military campaign decisions, sorcery, and even royal succession. Frequently multilingual and clearly familiar with a vast cornucopia of magical talents, the Old Women have been described as reciting spells in five different languages. Some certainly would also have had scribal skills. In their recorded rituals we have evidence of intentional dream incubation practice, the ritual banishment of nightmares, and the divine revelatory potential of spontaneous prophetic dreaming.

The Old Woman as sorceress knew how to invoke the sun goddess through rituals and incantations. She called to the sun goddess so that she would return to Earth and fulfill her duty of revivifying the plants and creatures. The Old Woman also operated bird and snake oracles in ritually prepared spaces. Oracles were extracted from the movements creatures made within demarcated arenas and their proximity to certain symbols. The Old Women were masters of the KIN, or action oracles, in which divination seems to have been practiced using a game board and symbolic tokens of some sort.[18]

We know also that supplicants could visit a temple of Ištar (a.k.a. Inanna) in Hittite times to receive divinely inspired dreams and visions from the goddess of love, beauty, sex, war, and justice. Ištar's dream-entering prowess is attested to in the Legend of Sargon,[19] a cuneiform tablet discovered in the library of the neo-Assyrian king Ashurbanipal. Prophetic dreams and visions of future greatness and divine protection were delivered by Ištar/Inanna to King Sargon, the founder of the Akkadian Empire. According to his legend, Sargon was the orphaned child of a priestess of Ištar who set the child adrift on the Euphrates.

In this Hittite text of an Old Woman ritual we can see an attempt to magically stop nightmares, which were believed to diminish one's life force. Although this text petitions the West Semitic Syrian dream-delivering deity El Kunirsha, this god is recognized by scholars as a version of the supreme Hittite god El, Creator (or Owner) of Earth, who becomes one of the major players in Hittite mythology.

They will place the large [di]sh on the ritual patron's lap, while he/she will t[ie(?)] rope(s) to [his left and(?)] his right hand.

The Old Woman libates one pit[cher of wi]ne for El-Kunirsha and says: O El-[Kunir]sha, Lord of the Dream/Sleep, son of the Dark Earth, husband/brother of the Sun-goddess of the Earth, deliverer! If the Sun-goddess of the Earth were for some reason angry with the ritual patron and she called upon you(?) for him and she called the innocent and the pure [ ]. . . for him,
either, whether he had made the Sun-God [of Heaven?] angry,

Or whether she was taking revenge(?) on him [for] his [ ] and she called upon you,
O El-Kunirsa for him. [And you], O El Kunirsha, Lord of the Dream/Sleep, evil dreams, evil shortened years, shortened months, shortened days [in a . . .] of lead
[ ] . . . will hold in front of him. Or if forth(?) [to him] the [gre]en(?) and the dark *munduwanda,*
. . . [. . .] the wolf, the fox, the snake and the scorpion you will hold out [for him].

[If however   ] you hold forth the plague(?) and . . .
isha[ra-sickness(?)]
[that] he/she may perform an invocation-ritual for
me and then . . .[   ]
[shortened] years, shortened months [shortened days]
[. . . . .] the wolf, the fox, the snake [and the scorpion]

Translated by Meindert Dijkstra[20]

MAGICAL MIRRORS

Of the tools and symbols employed by the Anatolian Old Women for magico-ritual purposes, mirrors and spindles are among the most fascinating. The spindle and mirror are both early symbols of womanhood, of female creative power and sexuality. They are frequently found together in female graves and are often incorporated into reliefs depicting powerful women. Together, the mirror and spindle are recorded as being the magical implements required by the sorceress for healing male impotence and belittling future enemies with ritual acts. With a spindle, a woman weaves together the fabric of reality. There is also the idea that the female is responsible for measuring out a certain allotment of life as a length of thread. With a mirror, that reality, and that portioned-out life, can be augmented according to her will.

These symbols are especially relevant when discussing the transition of human and material culture and consciousness through the Chalcolithic and into the Bronze Age. Let's take the mirror as an example of a seemingly simple human technology that altered our view of self and that of the world around us. Before humans developed the know-how to produce smooth and flawless metallic or tektite surfaces, a reflection was something one might glimpse in bodies of water, the eyes of another, and perhaps in rare mineral facets. Nowadays we are so incredibly familiar with our own high-definition appearance that it is really very hard to imagine a world in which you don't know exactly what you look like. If you do not know exactly what you look like, how does your perception of self change? Was there then a sort of group awareness, a collective perception of observed features from which individual group members could somehow telepathically draw?

The reflections given back to us by natural surfaces are vague and changeable, shaped by the unique morphology and character of each surface. Such reflections may have been captivating for this reason, suggesting supernatural insight but also deepening that sense of connection to elemental forces—a peering into the living Earth. Likely the nature of other realms perceived in early mirrors would be further influenced by the type of raw materials used to produce the objects. If you consider the abysslike murkiness of the first obsidian mirrors of early Anatolia[21] and indeed the smoking mirrors of Aztec diviners, in contrast with the gold, copper, or bronze mirrors of Mesopotamia and Egypt, you might expect to see some of the characteristics of the otherworlds they were revealing to be somewhat aesthetically and sympathetically matched with the substance from which they were made. Such reflections may have inspired ideas about an amorphous, fluid self with an umbilical connection to a gestating world.

Once developed and perfected, mirrors immediately acquired divinatory and ritual function. In ancient Egypt they were associated with birth and rebirth, and of course they were tools for future visions all over the ancient world. *Captromancy* is the name given to divination using a mirror, from the Greek κάτοπτρον/*katoptron,* "mirror," and μαντεία/*manteia,* "divination." As an ancient mirror reflected the world, it was seen to capture or contain a version of it, one that went beyond the boundaries of the mirror's physical dimensions and was subject to magical influence. Mirrors were among the world's first and most important magical treasured objects and are frequently found as part of the grave goods of elite members of many ancient societies.

If we take the capturing of self-image to its ultimate twenty-first-century zenith, we can track a strange return of the increasingly vague and nonaccurate reflections of our ancient ancestors. We have passed through a strata of high definition and are now in a domain of veils and filters that once again conceal and blur our true image. Our self-image can be frozen in time, animated, and transferred into alternate realities.

We can render images that are beyond the scope of human vision and reach. Not only can we now permanently capture an image of ourselves, but that image is also meshed within an etheric dimension and nested into our own material reality. We can now reproduce the infinitesimally small and the mind-bogglingly distant. We present ourselves chiefly as we wish to be seen. For now we see through a glass darkly. How truly do we relate to this curated self-image on a personal level? And how do these new technological innovations augment our ideas about who we are? Perhaps this is another indicator of our reorientation toward the oracular and magical.

A good example of the power of material culture to influence consciousness is a psychiatric disorder that developed in the fifteenth century. It came about in response to glass manufacturing and the increased use of the material in the homes of the wealthy. The "glass delusion" was a condition that made people feel like they were made out of glass and could splinter or shatter in a moment.[22] King Charles VI of France was a famous sufferer of this debilitating condition. He wouldn't let people touch him and wore specially made fortified outfits to protect himself from shattering. So this begs the questions: To what extent do we relate to our lived experience of being in a body, of existing within a particular environment, and to what degree does our sense of self rely on our mental projection into the image of that body that we see in mirrors, glass, photographs, and films? Are we already existing as avatars of ourselves? The plethora of options for self-representation the modern world now offers up is nothing short of overwhelming. Does this scattering of self-image mean that our conscious perception of self is in a fragmented and degraded state? Could this be a contributing factor to the contemporary prevalence of disassociation, anxiety, and depression? As a child, and as an exercise in boredom, I used to spend a lot of time looking into a mirror, observing my face, cultivating a trance state, and watching my face transform into that of a stranger. Here I could see that the self was a carefully, self-maintained illusion. In lucid dreams, the illusion of personality is palpable, and it is possible to experience an awareness of the world originating in the mind, directly.

Initiatic Story: Death in Anatolia

This feels right. I am surrounded, as if I am a granule packed into a crystal's lattice. Oh, the safety, the concentration, the focus of this collection of souls and moving bodies—it just feels right.

I feel now the movements of every body within this gridded settlement, a settlement delineated by squarish earthen cells, by roof terraces canopied by woven grass shades, and by roughly hewn wood stakes. This stake here, for example, is topped by a bunting, a bunting hunting for ants, grubs, and the glittering beetle bodies that scuttle around its labyrinths, the beetles that lay their beautiful, identically transparent eggs in its hollows.

From where I am now I can feel this stake, I can feel its fibers warmed by the sun. I can feel the blunt protrusions worn smooth by the elements, rotting in pockets. I can feel the probing, curious, short, and stout beak of the bunting. I can feel the dodging beetles, determined ants, and tender, wriggling grubs.

From the top of this stake I can feel the one who is crouched down beside the stream, scraping a fox skin with his obsidian blade. I can feel the keenness of the blade edge and the eager grooves in the flesh of man and fox. I can feel the gobbets of fat and muscle as they curdle against the knife. As the lumps are torn away, sinews ripping, I can feel their stretchy threads clinging to my fingers. In the dark mirror of a facet in chipped obsidian, I can see the energy passing through the hands and thumbs of the new grandmother as she carefully plasters the skull of the old grandmother with bloodied mud. From the eyeless sockets of the old grandmother's skull, I can see the naked children rolling in the dirt and sharp grass with their dogs . . .

In this fever I am drenched in sweat and shivering. My teeth are chattering like oracle bones jumping in a bowl, and I wonder if they speak of my future. So I try to listen to their prophetic rhythm. While I am paralyzed by this internal fire, my poisoned blood boiling up in me, my dreaming body is traveling far away. Part of me is birdlike, part of me is a bunting hunting for ants. With my flying eyes, I seek out

Grandmother in the shrine and I find her. I hear her breathing, and then I hear her singing voice.

First I see only the back of her. She is rocking forward and backward slightly, as if pulled and pushed by a spirit. She is wrapped loosely in spotted brown furs, her ashen hair twisted with clay. Then my vision becomes more complete and she turns to face me. Her visage is truly incredible. Her face deeply lined, like tree bark or the texture of unworked deer hide. Her hair is all tubules of green snakes. These thin snakes have clear yellow eyes; they look like silver water droplets on a lily pad.

The snakes move as one. They rotate their scaly neck bodies and hiss at me. Now I notice the low hum of many bees coming from deep within the old woman's rib cage. Her breath is sweet and sickly. Bees crawl out of her mouth. She drools honey and crushes the comb with her pitted gums as she grins. Her eyes are bone-white cowrie shells. Gray-frilled tongues slime out to lick her dead-looking eyelids. Now I can see she holds the head of the old grandmother in her hands. Her hands are the talons of the vulture and they are caked in bloody mud . . .

The cheekless skull of the old grandmother laughs. Even with her withered scalp and her pathetic wisps of hair, she is full of mirth. This bubbling mirth is transmitted magically to me. Not just to me but also to the fabric of the world that eddies around us. On the wall behind her are the massive black faces of great horned beasts. They are coming to life with ridiculous laughter. They're flaring their nostrils and snorting and spluttering at the joke. Even the rumbling hearth leans back into an exhalation of hilarity. The hearth breathes soot onto the lime-washed walls . . .

The old grandmother puckers her ancient, parched lips. Her head lies in the lap and claws of the new grandmother. The new grandmother clutches the skull like a pearl. The old grandmother begs and bleats like a babe. Like a desperate baby, she demands milk from the new grandmother's breast.

In response, the old woman's sagging copper chest becomes lusty and fresh. Her breasts turn heavy and round with milk. Her tender nipples blossom with popping pink flower buds. A growing, bovine heaviness forces her onto her hands and knees. Her breasts are pooling now into a laden, fleshy udder that presses into the earth as it swells. Taloned fingers are digging into the ground. The head of the old grandmother feeds greedily from the new grandmother. She sucks furiously, even as her rotted old face is squashed under the gigantic bosom. The new grandmother cries with pain and pleasure. Her running veins ache with relentless life. With every violent tug at her nipple, with each gush of nourishing milk that comes forth, the old grandmother gains vitality.

The shell eyes in the old grandmother's skull begin to sparkle like perfect jewels. Her skin becomes beautiful, her painted face becomes radiant and serene. A divine glitter passes over her. I want her to take me. I want to give her everything. I desire her, I need to fill her with my seed. I see the eyes and mouths of a million future babies. I see the eyes and mouths of a million handsome and hideous old men and women. I surrender to her. I feel myself dissolve, to know the liquid ecstasy of her skull . . .

Things become blurry, as though I pass slowly behind a waterfall. I am now bathing in a vast pool of warm milk. I am inside a dark red, echoing cave. The pool is filled with large silver fishes. They have square jaws, short fins, and thick black lines down their bodies. They squirt jets of water through their mouths at me. I am swirling around with them. We are pushing up against the edges as we lap against the inside of this cave. I feel the long scrape of sandy stone walls. My naked body is carried by a sure, spiraling current. It is jostled by giant fish that circle into nothingness. The current draws me closer to the middle of the pool. It is impossible to fight the flow, so I am going with the flow. Now in the center of the pool, a gathering sun is rising. Its corona is steaming. Its vapors are intoxicating; the whole cavernous chamber fills with murk . . .

I am melting into warm milk. The warm milk sucks me toward the heart of the molten orb. I understand that the milk belongs to a mind and it has a soul. The milk is a living fluid. It is the fluid of memory. When I think of its heart, I feel its pulse and it slows to know me. We pulse together so that I may also know it. The color of the milk begins turning—first to pink and then to the red of fresh blood. The sun swallows me. I am drawn into the white light of eternity at its core. It pulls me down into the earth and I am lost in fantasy. I am a serpent devouring its own tail, turning inside out. The earth drinks me in . . .

I feel a deep wash of peace. It radiates in and out of some blazing kernel within me. My reduction, my essence. Bliss is flooding my senses, joy is blinding me. I actually attempt to bellow with joy, but my voice is utterly silent. A pitch blackness rolls out before me. Lines of light form in this abyss. Through a prism of invisible tears, infinite weird worlds and astonishing, alien visions rush at me. I see impossible ways of being. I see all the ways I have been before. I see flashes of unknowable ancient histories. I can hear whistling, the melodic languages of the future. I can hear the answer to a question. And then I hear the question.

I say, "Yes!"
She says, "Will you come?"

I feel myself unfolding into something eternal. I am obliterated by how much I adore the Earth and how much she adores me. She thinks I am delicious, and all I want to do is feed her my beating heart. I am enraptured. She wants me back . . .

The light of my life in the world is snuffed out. I am dismembered. I am remembered. I am returned. Returned to the stars. I sparkle in a sea of endless sky, and I am one with the swimming fishes of all other souls. I can now hear the pure harmony of Heaven. I have now transcended the chaos and cacophony of worldliness. I know the beginning and end of all things. I know there is a new dawn. This feels right.

Dream Writing and Ritual

The Ancient Near East

3300 to 1200 BCE

O Gula, sublime lady, merciful mother,
Among the myriad stars of the heavens,
O lady, to you I turn; my ears are attentive to you.
Receive my flour offering, accept my prayer.
Let me send you to my angry (personal) god (and) my angry (personal) goddess,
To the god of my city who is furious and enraged with me.
On account of oracles and dreams that are hounding me,
I am afraid and constantly anxious.
O Gula, most exalted lady, through the word of your august command, which is supreme in Ekur,
And your sure approval, which cannot be altered,
May my furious god turn back to me; may my angry goddess turn again to me with favor.
May the god of my city who is furious and enraged with me,

Audio track 3, "Threshold," is the companion to this phase.

Who is in a rage, relent; who is incensed, be soothed.
O Gula, most exalted lady, who intercedes on behalf of the
powerless,
With Marduk, king of the gods, merciful lord,
Intercede! Speak a favorable word!
May your wide canopy (of protection), your noble
forgiveness be with me.
Provide a requital of favor and life for me,
That I may proclaim your greatness (and) resound your
praises!

FROM *AKKADIAN PRAYERS AND HYMNS:*
A READER, TRANSLATED BY ALAN LENZI

The Mesopotamian culture of Sumer, traditionally credited for having invented writing, took existing star lore and transformed folk wisdom into a formal textual and illustrated discipline. The evolving art of astronomy was already closely associated with divinely initiated dreaming. As we shall see, the magic potential of dreams were influenced by divine star beings who were best accessed after sunset, when the brilliance of the firmament gains full magnitude.

In the Sumerian language, the stars are *šitir šame,* the "writing of Heaven."[1] According to Paleolithic beliefs, the stars were a language in themselves, one that could be read to determine the future. During the Neolithic, the chief function of this star knowledge was to act as an efficient agricultural almanac and cosmic calendar for communal planning and survival. The Stone Age acquisition and dissemination of star information was essentially a pragmatic pursuit, although no doubt infused with reverence for a natural order and an underlying faith in some sort of spiritual cosmic reality. The cultures of the Near East, including those of Sumer, Assyria, Akkadia, and Babylon, subsequently expanded this discipline to include more specific prescriptions for medicine to address various ailments and to assist in prophecy, festival time-keeping, and all sorts of other ritual activities.

With the development of astral knowledge, the gods now had opportunities to connect with a person's life on an intimate and unprecedented scale. The stars could helpfully reveal whether a person was favored or scorned by their all-important personal gods, the gods allocated to them at birth. This blessing or disdain by personal gods ultimately dictated a person's state of health and well-being. If you annoyed your gods somehow, the gods could visit nightmares upon you, and a nightmare at this time in human history might be considered a demonic etheric entity with its own volition. As a result, the impersonal nature of the bad dream made people especially terrified of inauspicious and frightening dream encounters. For this reason, deities associated with beneficent dreams and healing were sought out by the sufferers of nightmares to placate personal gods on their behalf. These dream deities, usually goddesses, could not only win back the favor of a person's personal gods, but they could also identify what faux pas had caused the gods to take umbrage with them in the first place. And they could tell the querent exactly what course of action to take to secure their forgiveness.

Prophecy was also a gift of the goddesses and gods of the underworld who presided over Mesopotamian dream rituals, and these deities were often credited with supplying illumination to those wandering through the underworld, called the Great Below. Wanderers through this realm were privy to underworld secrets of the yet-to-unfold day. So the Great Below, as well as being a zone explorable in special dreams, was a realm associated with special portents, as well as a place of regeneration, Earth magic, and medicine.

ASTRAL IRRADIATION

Assyriologist Erica Reiner makes a case for a sort of "astral irradiation" being employed by ancient Mesopotamian spirit doctors as a way of healing the sick with starlight power. She describes how a charm, amulet, herb, magic potion, or even a whole sick body might be bathed in starlight, the idea being that the person would absorb heavenly influences and the beneficent, healing emanations of the stars, the "gods of the night."[2] To bathe in the heavenly radiance of the firmament would indeed be potent magic. At the touch of their light, through the reach of their divine rays, the gods of the night could infuse a sleeping patient with healing power, and they could vastly increase the efficacy of any appeal, spell, charm, or medicine. The stars are a balm in the blanket of the night sky, and act as a most potent panacea.

Prayers to the star gods would often include the divine names of rivers, too. The waters of Earth were seen as reflecting the luminous heavens. These vital, serpentine forces at night contained an aspect of the star gods. Touched by gods, this water could be considered divine, because it provided holy sustenance to the land and its people and pure, celestially sanctified waters for purification rites.

DOG GODDESS AND DREAM HEALER

The dog goddess Gula, a Mesopotamian goddess of medicine, usually depicted with a dog, emerged during the Old Babylonian Empire. She seems to have intertwined with the earlier goddess figures Baba (Bawa) and Bau, who were also protective, healing dog deities of Sumer and Akkad. Some believe the name Bau/Bawa/Baba to be onomatopoeic, an attempt to mimic, French-style, the *bowwow* of a dog's bark. Dogs had for a long time already been recognized as creatures of healing, domestication, and protection. A real reverence and appreciation for dogs had been cultivated through the close companionship, coevolution, and cooperation between humans and dogs since the Paleolithic.

Early humans would certainly have observed the healing effect of dog saliva on wounds, so there is reason to believe dogs may have been incorporated into prehistoric healing practices. Dog saliva is known to facilitate the speedy healing of wounds and promote new tissue growth. It even has antimicrobial and antibacterial properties. Human saliva works as well, but humans are generally less enthusiastic about its application—although at least they usually refrain from licking their own buttholes!

Dogs are, of course, excellent guardians and defenders of humans. With their keen senses and dogged, at times even violent loyalty, they are especially useful when humans are asleep. They were likely the very first animal attendants to the first dreamers who took part in incubation rituals in the earliest purposefully constructed dream shrines and sleep temples. Dogs continued to be animal assistants even in the healing sleep temples of the late Hellenic and Roman periods. For example, many votive dog statues, images, and offerings have been unearthed at the remains of the Temple of Nodens, a Romano-British site overlooking the river Severn, in the Forest of Dean, England. The temple and the Celtic deity Nodens were associated with dream revelations, healing, curses, and miracle-working. Onsite dogs may have provided soothing licks as a real-world treatment to wounded supplicants.

It is now accepted by modern science that the tremendous olfactory organs of dogs—they possess up to 300 million olfactory receptors in their noses, compared to our sniffling 6 million[3]—can help them smell certain illnesses, even sometimes in very early stages, when undetectable by modern medicine's conventional tests. Anecdotally, dogs are perceived by many people to have strange powers of precognition and frequently of imminent or not-so-imminent death. Dogs have often been observed choosing to sit in the lap of particular people in residential homes, and it is often observed that those people might be the closest to death. So this is another element that leads us to contemplate a canine predisposition for divination. Dog owners frequently talk about their pet's ability to know the future, to sense an unexpected arrival, or to respond to an invisible presence or future threat. Dogs are portrayed as chthonic entities or guardians in many ancient belief systems. As such, they would also be seen as having special access to the future worlds of humans.

QUEEN OF ANIMALS

The impulse to tame and domesticate animals in early human populations really set the tone for how future cultures and belief systems evolved. A preference for domestication, for control, and a conscious division between that which is wild or chaotic and that which is ordered, is really the foundation of all creation myths and spiritual systems. This dividing line is a crack in the bedrock reality that creates a duality and a chasm through which all of the gods of the unknown could escape.

A tame dog exemplifies the pacification of chaotic and wild forces, which is what illness and disease were considered to be in ancient Mesopotamia. The dog therefore makes a perfect symbol for healing and harmonious integration. Images of Gula and her dogs could be considered examples of the *Potnia Theron,* or Mistress of Animals, motif, one of the most widespread images in the corpus of ancient symbolic art. The Mistress of Animals is perhaps the archetype of a tamer or domesticator. It's a motif that pops up throughout the Mediterranean, Anatolia, and the Indus Valley; in fact, it appears everywhere, in particular alongside the domestication of animals and the beginnings of agricultural life. We can imagine this image of the Mistress of Animals as one that memorialized a cultural shift toward dominion over the natural order, an image made mythological by the increasingly sedentary, world-building descendants of ancient nomadic peoples.

But sometimes for protection, an ancestral, ancient, untamed wildness is required, is in fact absolutely necessary. When invoked for protection, Gula could be fierce, like so many of the archetypal healer goddesses of antiquity. She was as fearless as her dog attendants were when defending her family, and she had the power to subdue the febrile chaos of disease. Like a dog, Gula was a strong, useful, benevolent, and protective companion to have throughout life.

Gula's male consort is usually Ninurta, an agricultural god associated with healing, justice, and the scribal arts. Ninurta also had the power to release humans from the bonds of sickness. He chased away the demons who caused imbalance, those evil spirits who could steal away a person's energy reserves. He could also release victims from a demon's nefarious clutches. In the epic poem *Exploits of Ninurta,* he is depicted as a giant striding over the land, cleaving the possessed mountain of the demon Azag. When Ninurta releases the great rivers of Mesopotamia, he initiates the original irrigation of the land for its people. Ninurta, then, is also a landscape gardener, a cultivator, and a tamer of the elements—in short, a domesticator of wildness in service of humanity.

As humans continued to domesticate, segregate, modify, and manage the many animal and plant populations with which they had previously mingled more inconspicuously, perhaps they started to wonder if they themselves were subject to domestication by invisible powers from above or below. As they began to compartmentalize all things, including space and time, creating thresholds, ritual calendars, and increasingly complex domiciles and communal buildings, they increasingly differentiated between wild and tame beasts, people, and places. They began to delineate gender roles more reservedly, too, to classify and grade attributes and weaknesses. As they manipulated the features of their own environments, perhaps they began to wonder: who was manipulating *them*.

THE DOG HOUSE

The *é-gal-mah* (Exalted House) temple at Isin in southern Mesopotamia (today the archaeological site Ishan al-Bahriyat in southern Iraq) was the seat of Gula's cult.[4] Within this temple complex was the *é-ur-giz-ra*, or Dog House. Dozens of dog burials have been discovered under the ramp leading into Gula's temple. Similar dog burials are located throughout the Levant and across the Eastern Mediterranean, where it is believed that Gula's influence spread.

Ceremonial dog burial in the ancient world was a fairly widespread practice, and in Mesopotamia it could certainly be in part due to the association with Bau/Gula. Perhaps this dictated taboos around eating dog flesh, too. There was also a taboo about eating flamingoes, which were considered the unclean birds of Gula[5] (although later the Romans developed a few tasty flamingo recipes, and they apparently especially relished that bird's tongue).

The chief activity of temple workers at Gula's Dog House seems to have been feeding and caring for dogs, many of which appear to have lived to a ripe old age, even with some having long-term albeit tended-to injuries. Gula's temple served primarily as a healing sanctuary for humans. Cures of all sorts were performed, from ritualized dream incubation with the intention of receiving a spontaneous divine cure or prescription to the petitioning of a supplicant's personal gods. A cure might be delivered by the use of sympathetic or prophylactic magic. Treatments also included more traditional methods of amelioration, such as surgery, wound cleansing and dressing, sleep, herbal remedies, fumigations, fasting, purification, and possibly even hirudotherapy (the application of medicinal leeches).[6]

MEDICAL PRACTICES IN ANCIENT MESOPOTAMIA

In Mesopotamia, responsibility for health care was often split between the workings of a physician, known as an *azu,* and a spirit doctor, the *ašipu.* Both parties might conclude that a weakness or illness has a supernatural or outside cause, but the azu worked exclusively with the physical body, offering herbal remedies, surgery, compresses, fumigations, and other physical procedures to minimize suffering. The azu underwent a medical apprenticeship at the temples of Gula, which were dedicated to the healing arts. In these temples, educational textbook tablets were studied, regular rounds with an experienced physician were observed as part of an induction, and the novice azu was given ample opportunity for supervised practice on patients.

The medical practitioners of Mesopotamia were familiar with a vast and complex pharmacopeia. They used antiseptics, analgesics, astringents, laxatives, and narcotics, including opium poppy, cannabis, mandrake, darnel (poison ryegrass), and hemlock (which is believed by some to have been combined with opium poppy to perform euthanasia, a ritual that would likely have been the domain of the ašipu).[7]

The ašipu, or spirit doctor, worked with more subtle, invisible forces, sorcery, and magic. They used charms, divination, and religious incantations to ward off the nefarious influences that were causing disease, with the main objective being appeasement of the patient's personal gods and the elicitation of renewed psychic protection from them.

Negative influences made themselves known through omens and portents and were often revealed in terrifying nightmares and bad dreams. As in many worldviews in antiquity, gods and the dead were able to communicate with, punish, or restore mortals to health and happiness in their dreams. Much importance was attached to the ašipu's ability to work out the initial offense that the person had committed. Another class of practitioner was the *baru,* a diviner who could read omens in the entrails and livers of ritually sacrificed animals. A baru might be brought in for prognoses and omens. An evocation of the sort of oracular consciousness that held sway in Mesopotamia at the time that refers to the typical work of a baru is nicely summarized by the Sumerian king Shulgi when he writes, "In the insides of a single sheep, I, the king, can find the messages for the whole universe."[8] (Translated from the Sumerian by Irving Finkel, Ph.D., in his book *The Ark Before Noah: Decoding the Story of the Flood*).

The meticulously kept records of Gula's Dog Temple at the Sumerian city-state Isin provide precise evidence of the activities conducted within its walls, as well as accounts of the vast amount of food and provisions the temple dogs received. The temple was a site of holy pilgrimage. Many supplicants would have visited Gula's temple in search of healing, auspicious dreams, advice, protection, and blessings.

The name Gula derives from the Sumerian language, and its root means "great," "increase," or "abundance." Her epithets include Great Physician, Great Healer, *Azugallatu* (in Sumerian, "great healer") of the Land of the Black-Headed Ones (the Sumerians), and Herb Grower. In Akkadian medical incantations the goddess is referred to as *Bēlit balāti,* "Lady of Health" or "Mistress of Life."[9] Gula is associated with the Babylonian constellation the She-Goat, known as UZA. UZA is the constellation Lyra on modern astronomical maps. An astral component to the goddess can be traced back to Gula's earliest roots. The brightest star in the She-Goat/Lyra constellation is Vega, which was known to Sumerian astronomers as Lamma, messenger of the goddess and Gula's dog-goddess-precursor Baba.[10]

As a patron guardian of the Sumerian city-state Isin, Gula was Ninisinna, Lady of Isin, and was syncretized with the goddess Inanna, Queen of Heaven, who came to be the premier Mesopotamian goddess. Inanna eventually assimilates the healing prowess of Gula; she even commandeers her canine companions, who become her pack of hunting dogs. In Inanna's Akkadian manifestation as Ištar, the goddess is invoked for dream assistance and has a reputation for oneiric consultations at her temples in Babylon.

Eshmun and Asklepios

Gula is known to have had other temples, at Borsippa, Aššur, and Nippur, in what is present-day Iraq. The energy of her cult appears to have been adopted at later healing dream sanctuaries, and this assured the continued employment of her healing temple dogs. Dogs were an important feature of healing sanctuaries, even into ancient Greece, being considered one of the animal, or theriomorphic forms, alongside snakes, of the god Greek god of medicine, Asklepios. Dogs were also commonly found in temples dedicated to the goddesses Astarte, Aphrodite, and Hekate.

The famous Greek dream healer god Asklepios, whom we shall explore in more detail later on, may have inherited his chthonic regenerative power from the earlier Phoenicians and Canaanites of the Levant. The Phoenicians worshipped a god of healing and vegetation known as Eshmun, who originated in an area near the modern-day city of Beirut. Eshmun became syncretized with Asklepios in Hellenized Phoenicia, when the Persian Empire ceded to Alexander the Great. At this time, the sacred grove around Eshmun's temple at Sidon became known as the Grove of Asklepios.

In the beautiful village of Bterram, in El Koura, northern Lebanon, there is an ancient underground temple in a Phoenician sanctuary called Eshmunit, made up of eight chambers, one large and seven small—perhaps for dream incubation? These rooms are carved into solid bedrock, accessible by steps. It is thought that this temple was dedicated to a consort of Eshmun, perhaps even an Etruscan-influenced version of the Phoenician/Canaanite goddess Astarte known as Turan.

NANŠE, GODDESS OF DREAM DIVINATION

"If a man cannot remember the dream he sees,
(then it means:) his personal god is angry with him."
—Old Babylonian OmThis en, Tablet VAT 7525.
Translated by Franz Köcher,
A. L. Oppenheim, and H. G. Güterbock

The Sumerian goddess Nanše was the daughter of the Creatrix goddess Ninḫursaĝ and the god of wisdom, magic, and water, Enki. Like her father, Nanše was also associated with water, wisdom, and prophecy. Enki is credited with defining the correspondences between Earth's fauna, flora, and minerals, as well as the mapping of the human anatomy. This divine divinatory blueprint becomes the basis of much of the quintessentially Mesopotamian medical methodology practiced by healers in Gula's sanctuaries, as well as Nanše's oracular temples. Medical prognoses were often based on dream revelations, divination, and the ability to read signs and omens in the living human or sacrificed animal body and natural phenomena in the surrounding environment.

Nanše ruled over the Persian Gulf, including all the avian and aquatic life that dwelled in the water, as well as the fishing communities that depended on it for their livelihood. Her familiars were the goose, the pelican, and the fish. Nanše was sometimes referred to as the Lady of the Store Houses, as she presided over weights, measures, and agricultural abundance. She was seen to swell beer pots to overflowing; grain baskets and coffers of all kinds became rich and heavy under her influence. Nanšes had close association with dream interpreters and skilled dreamers. She acted as a mediator between the gods and mortals, relaying divinely sent messages through coherent dream interpretation.

Nanše's functionaries received training in an established Mesopotamian dream interpretation tradition, which included consideration of the personal conditions, health, and status of the dreamer and some familiarity with a stock of dream texts. Dreams are the subject of a wide variety of ancient Mesopotamian textual material, including letters, prayers, magic, incantations, medicine, oracular writings, literary texts and royal inscriptions. The dream book *Iškar Zaqīqu*, "Core Text of the God Zaqīqu" was discovered in the Library of Ashurbanipal in ancient Ninevah, modern-day Mosul in northern Iraq. This dream compendium, written in the Akkadian language, consists of eleven cuneiform tablets. The text is believed to have been copied from a Babylonian original and contains dream interpretation, deductive divination, and rituals for the banishment of bad dreams. *Zaqīqu*, or *Sisig* in Sumerian, is a word for a ghost or spirit, but when written with the determinative symbol for a god or divine entity, Sisig manifests as the offspring of the Sumerian sun god Utu and becomes a divine personification of a dream, one that travels as personified spirit breeze. So, in the case of this Sisig, a dream in the Mesopotamian consciousness can literally *be* a god spirit. Initiation rites required Nanše's operatives to go through a symbolic death and rebirth, which concluded their apprenticeship and bestowed on them divine prophetic abilities. As prophecy was associated with the underworld, the chthonic realm of the dead, it was perhaps necessary to symbolically die and travel through the underworld before you could know the future.

Sometimes her dream priests were referred to as "Cupbearers." In ancient Mesopotamia, Cupbearer is an honorific title usually bestowed on a supremely trusted, high-ranking officer who was responsible for pouring out drinks at the royal court. Cuneiform tablets mention priests preparing ritual beverages. Perhaps in the context of Nanše's temple this suggests that there was some mild mind-altering substance being used and that a sufficiently high dose of whatever it was might result in the initiatory, temporary, deathlike experience required by her neophytes. An infusion of opium, Syrian rue, mandrake, henbane, or darnel—all spiritually endowed plants familiar to the ašipu—could have been used for this purpose.

Nanše's temples had a secondary function as places of refuge for orphans, refugees, debtors, and widows. In her social justice role, the goddess was defender of the innocent, the vulnerable, the lost, and all manner of underdogs. These religious sanctuaries were places to sleep and rest without the threat of peril, places for protected dreaming. The sanctuaries were believed to have been bestowed on the goddess by the Abzu, the mythological body of freshwater beneath the land that had fertilizing and purifying qualities. Nanše would materialize within the walls of her consecrated temple in the evening. Those who came seeking her blessing, a dream interpretation, or a prophetic vision hoped to receive it when they slept or rested within the temple complex. I wonder if this represents an acknowledgment of something like the dream-within-a-dream experience. If it was necessary to meet Nanše in the dream realm to have a previous dream interpreted by her, this shows a layering of conscious dream awareness. Her counsel offered wisdom and instruction for action.

DREAM DEMON LILITH

In ancient Sumer, supernatural beings were a real part of the fabric of reality. They traveled on winds both ill and favorable. Because of this association with the element of air, spirits could be conjured up or exorcised using the holy smoke of incense.

In the Sumerian mythological story "Inanna and the Huluppu Tree," related in the preamble to the *Epic of Gilgamesh,* which tells of the odyssey of Gilgamesh, king of the Mesopotamian city-state Uruk, Inanna identifies the World Tree, which connects Heaven and Earth on the banks of the Euphrates. She brings the World Tree to her holy garden at Uruk, where she tends it for many years, intending to carve it into a shining throne and make a fine bed for herself. In doing so she hopes to establish her sovereignty and dominion over the three realms of Heaven, Earth, and underworld. However, during this time some unwanted residents move in: the divine storm bird Anzû and its young, in the tree's branches; the serpent who knows no charm and is immune to incantations, in the tree's roots; and Lilith, a phantom or dark maiden who embodies loneliness, emptiness, and the wildness of nature, who has taken up residence in the tree's trunk. Gilgamesh helpfully kills the snake with an ax, while the Anzû bird flies off to the mountains with its fledglings, and the phantom maiden Lilith flees to the wild, uninhabited places of the desert. In the Hebrew language the name Lilith (or the variations Lilit, Lillake, and Lilitu) is translated as "night creature," "night monster," "night hag," and "screech owl," and much like the ghostly apparition of an owl, the demon Lilith hunts on the wing at night for her compromised victims.

In the diabolical representations of Lilith as sketched out by the Hebrews in their Babylonian exile, she resembles the Mesopotamian demon goddess Lamaštu, who was similarly expelled from a paradisiacal realm. Both demonesses waged war on pregnant women and babies. If a child laughed in their sleep, it was an inauspicious sign that Lilith was playing with them.

Lilith became a demonic succubus implicated in human infidelities and unwholesome cravings. As such she would descend on hapless males in the night, drawing out their life force by giving them erotic dream visions. She would then harvest the nocturnal emissions of her witless victims to create a legion of vile demon offspring. As her sad, spent victims lay paralyzed in fevered wet dreams, she would drain them of their life-giving sap, sometimes to the point of death.

One can't help but wonder if Lilith became something of a psychic *tulpa,* a type of imaginal entity made manifest through spiritual or mental powers, as described by Theosophists.[11] Lilith was penned by the scribes, painted by artists, and rendered into spiral-patterned demon bowls by potters.[12] The demon bowl is a device, a simple bowl decorated with a spiraling prayer and image of Lilith at the center, designed to magically capture the demoness if she crossed the threshold of a dwelling. Lilith was greatly feared, spoken of in whispers, yet secretly craved in the imagination. Eventually she was admitted to the collective unconsciousness.

Initiatic Story: Threshold

The panicked horned viper sidewinded rapidly over the floor. She was sandy scaled and patterned with pinkish dune waveforms.

Tauthe found the undulating movements and sounds hypnotic. The snake's rapid body scribed *sssssssss* diagonally across the ground, its actions expanded and decelerated by the mesmerizing effects of the dream medicine now ensnaring Tauthe's senses. In real time, the serpent escaped within seconds, disappearing into a deep fracture in the hard-packed earth in the corner of the reed hut. Tauthe was to wait in this chamber for a prophecy, ear to the ground. The viper could now be heard moving more calmly and comfortably, her forked tongue tasting the way to the place of secrets. The horned goddess in her ophidian form was returning to the realm of dreams and death.

A cupbearer walked past the door, silver cups jangling on a cord tied at the waist. A trailing robe bristled against the long, loose reeds at the bottom of the doorpost. Tauthe took the cup, downed the last dregs it contained, and felt the gritty remains grate against teeth and tongue. The delicate impressions of water, fish, geese, and flying ducks that decorated the cup were beginning to take on a life of their own. They oscillated gently under Tauthe's watery, smoke-stung gaze. The ducks ruffled their feathers. The fish rippled their fins and glistened their scales. Everything was now synchronizing with the slowing rhythm of Tauthe's breathing . . .

The supplicants first bathed in the living water of the river before entering the reed temple complex to expose themselves to the aqueous fingers of the gods. When they emerged, they were wrapped in clean white linen sheets and ritually fumigated with cedarwood and juniper. Their hands, faces, eyes, and mouths were purified by the water of the Abzu, which flowed into the temple font.

Attendants drew a protective boundary to mark out the sacred space by pouring a long, curving line of flour. The altar was framed by two bigger-than-life-size idols of divine females. These figures were carved from the trunks of two massive and ancient tamarisk trees. Offerings of doves, sparrows, and fish were left for the goddesses. Engraved votives, inscribed vessels, and cut jewels like wet, translucent fruit, dripped their sparkles on the altar.

The holy statues were bathed, carefully dried, draped in the finest linen, and anointed with perfumed sesame oil infused with cardamon, cinnamon, cassia, saffron, and myrrh. Their silent mouths were tempted open by honeycomb, ghee, and cypress resin. They were veiled in sacred smoke, their smoothly shining limbs criss crossed with ropes of articulated electrum and beaded vines of finely hammered, pressed gold leaves. Diadems were set on their heads—fragile gold star points and paper-thin, delicately veined petals clasped luminous gems of chalcedony and agate, polished carnelian, lapis lazuli, and banded jasper. Garlands of flowers were placed around oiled necks and breasts—heavenly scented heavy blossoms of pink wild roses, purple-barbed irises, white lilies laden with pollen, and oxeye daisies. Everything oozed life. The sap was rising . . .

Crystal eyes inlaid with the blackest onyx stone for pupils glittered in the beams of sunlight that broke into the temple enclosure. These beams impaled the clouds of smoke rising from the incense burning in the brazier. Glowing spears were suspended in midair. The colors throbbed. Priests recited hymns to the statues. Many initiates fell to their knees, their eyes shining wet with tears. They were showered by the Abzu droplets that spiraled out of shaking pinecones. All of this was an invitation to vivify the statues.

Fine, white, feathery fish bones curled and blackened in the fierce fire at the altar's hearth. The cupbearers distributed silver cups to the neophytes. A priestess poured out the dreaming drafts from a consecrated vase. She whispered an incantation over the flowing potion as it filled each cup. Inanna was the goddess of the threshold. Nanše the goddess of dream divination. The cupbearers sang hymns to the goddesses.

The temple was arranged to contain the seven realms, and the initiates came to pass over the thresholds of each of them. They entered the sacred precinct at sunrise. A small reed chamber was the place for the ultimate ritual as the sun set. This was the place for the little death with the sun god Šamaš, a dream that would transport one to the Great Below. This was the final realm from which the initiated returned renewed, unafraid of death, infused with the radiance of Inanna, and endowed with the future knowledge of Nanše . . .

Tauthe lay down to incubate, now naked and supine on the bed, a thick mat of woven reeds atop a raised bank of earth, covered in a coarse linen blanket, listening for the now distant serpent, witnessing the dimming of the world. With each increasingly lingering blink, a darkening . . . blinking, sinking, sinking, blinking, sinking, into stillness . . . a paralyzing, thick, drugged sleep . . . the medicine of Nanše sending the spirit down with the darkening sun, deep into the earth, the bodiless realm of potential actions and events . . .

Slipping through the fibers of flax, of split reeds, grains of earth, and splinters of stone, Tauthe traveled through all of their memories, too, their many past and parallel lives. Memories of the threshing circle. Remembrances of spirited breezes, swirling through golden fields of ripe linseed. Of the sudden flurry and flap of a startled night heron at the edge of a lake. The blunted slap of umber river water against the grooved hull of a reed boat. All their future incarnations, too, shaking, smacking, unraveling, the laughing voices of children, saturation, licks of flame and blackening blood, disintegration . . .

Like heavy, weighted smoke, Tauthe now followed the infinitely regenerating tail of the serpent into the underworld. Earthly life evaporated, all deeds swallowed up, trickling like water into darkness, the silver cup falling through the air and ringing with the memory of a bell . . .

The gateposts ahead were luminous, standing alone in the darkness. Beyond them was an abyss of light-sucking blackness. Weak threads of light were drawn into it magnetically. Weightless and formless, that which had been Tauthe now surrendered all energy to the void. Time vanished.

After aeons, perhaps, a sensation of landing heavily on the ground . . . In this ophidian and obsidian-lensed realm, new eyes were opened, all over. Tauthe was now bejeweled with astonished serpent's eyes, an all-seeing form. Everything moving, everything snaking, morphing, transforming, the very earth coiled and stretched . . . There came no light from a sun, nor stars, nor flame, but light seemed to escape from the pores of all things, and it had a violet-blue tinge, like cold fire.

There were huge, long-legged birds and gemmed insects. Tauthe felt a deep, reverberating silence. And there was Inanna, towering, terrifying, her visage frightening. The cold flames of the underworld were pouring violently around her body, the flames producing an aura of dark radiance. This was an absorbing antilight that made everything else darker around it. Tauthe trembled at Inanna's awesome countenance. Feline shadows prowled around the goddess's clawed feet. Lions and panthers paced and circled, serpents slithered toward her, attracted by her power, and their underworld energies fed her. There was so much power here, and that power balanced on a blade edge between chaos and control . . .

Inanna stepped onto the back of a giant lioness. The creature's lithe spine bowed underfoot. Tauthe saw the moisture on the cat's fangs, the follicles of her whiskers. Her vision permitted her to see all things from all places. She could see individual cells yet at the same time was able to observe some distance into the gloom. Inanna drew all of the world's serpents up and over her body. She threaded them through her fingers. The *shugurra,* the undulating crown of the steppe, rose on top of her head. A vast swathe of land crested and pasture folded over. In this moment she made the world of humans. In this moment she was the navel of the Earth. In this moment she was the all-powerful female, the Creatrix. She penetrated the male in this mirror realm. Her toes were the black talons of death that pierced the flesh. Her seed was a mnemonic germ, born from dismemberment and decay. The loops of nature wound all about her. All rose and fell, all lived and died through her body . . .

Doves burst through the vision, the soft white breasts of the birds pounding against Tauthe's million crystalline eyes. Like scales on the belly of a feathered serpent, they came without pause, all pure whiteness, their clamoring avian hearts desperate to escape the underworld. Tauthe saw their hearts now, beating in unison, like a beaded net of rubies intent on capturing the world of light. They were being called to adore Šamaš as he rose in the East. They were being called to make the joyful song of life and light to delight in earthly pleasures.

This singing called Tauthe back to the reed hut, to the temple. Called Tauthe back to a feeling form, the reeds vibrating, body flowing back to life like a river . . .

The flour was swept into a pile, thrown onto the fire. It turned black and became a winding gray spirit that went up to Heaven. The silver cup was slowly rolling still, still rolling slowly across the floor . . .

Phase Four

Temple Sleep and
Dream Sanctuaries

Ancient Egypt 3150 to 332 BCE

When a man dreams his own dream, he is the sport of his dream; when Another gives it him, that Other is able to fulfill it.

GEORGE MCDONALD, *LILITH*

Thousands of years ago, people all over the world were known to have engaged in an activity known as temple sleep. Sanctuaries, temples, and sometimes tombs were the sacred precincts of resident goddesses, gods, and the dead. These were special places where the divine would appear to mortals. Usually the deities and dead would manifest in dreams or as apparitions in other altered states.

In antiquity, those seeking healing, assistance, or oracles believed that sleeping in such places would facilitate a dream encounter with the god, goddess, or dead person associated with that particular sanctuary or tomb. In ancient Egyptian metaphysical thinking, aspects of a dead person's spirit or their immaterial essence—in particular their *ba* and *ka*[1]—were at times believed to return to the safe sanctuary of their

---

Audio track 4, "Eye," is the companion to this phase.

tomb and perfectly preserved body. This is why deceased persons were furnished with the most lavish and elaborate provisions they were able to afford in their lifetime. It is why ancient Egyptian funerary buildings were so often decked out with many items of luxury and comfort, including real and imaginary food and drink. This was the reason that the skillful art of mummification aimed to be so exacting in its preservation, because a person's body was seen as the earthly base of these spiritual components. The *ib,* the heart, was considered to be the vessel that held the spiritual essence of a person in both life and death.

While the dead person's brain was carefully discarded upon death (the ancient Egyptian word for *brain* translates into something like "skull offal"[2]) and the lungs, liver, intestines, and stomach were packed into magically protective canopic jars, the heart was carefully preserved, wrapped, and returned to the body. The heart was required as currency in the trials of the Duat, the ancient Egyptian otherworld. In the Duat, the heart was weighed against the feather of Ma'at, the goddess of balance, justice, and harmony. Because the heart was believed to be the seat of the soul, spirit, and intellect, it was vital that it did not perish and that the body, as the personally identified container for this spiritual organ, should likewise be preserved indefinitely. If the heart and body perished, the spiritual entities that dwelled inside them could be lost and obliterated from memory forever. Much of the essence of these beliefs still exists in the animistic folk traditions of many cultures that persist to this day in places such as Mexico and Russia; for example, activities such as taking food to the ancestors or sleeping on graves to communicate with the dead. These are ritual acts performed in the belief that they will keep the memory of a loved one or relative alive, as well as keep their disembodied spirits spiritually sated, and this echoes some of the principles of ancient Egypt's afterlife beliefs.

EGYPTIAN DREAM INCUBATION AND INTERPRETATION

There is very little textual or monumental evidence of dedicated dream incubation complexes in Egypt before the Greco-Roman period, which is when the Hellenic god of medicine, Asklepios, syncretized with the earlier Egyptian deified healer Imhotep. However, it is unlikely that such a widespread and well-documented practice was not taking place in some form or another in Egypt before that time. It is more likely that a form of temple sleep with elements of necromancy was a folk tradition connected to honoring ancestors. There was probably a widespread cultural understanding in predynastic times, and the practice therefore required no formal institutionalization. It's possible that the structured oracular culture of dreaming and dream interpretation was developed when the influence of other religious systems in the Near East merged with the private rituals of native ancestor worship.

Temple sleep as a ritual practice is frequently attested to in ancient Egyptian narrative texts and inscriptions. A divine dream might be solicited—asked for, prayed for, or requested—or it may come unsolicited, occurring spontaneously, particularly when the sleeper dozes at a site of godly power or is boozed-up at a festival of drunkenness. Egyptologist Kasia Szpakowska, who specializes in ancient Egyptian dreams, nightmares, and demonology, describes instances of such dream encounters with Hathor, goddess of the sky, women, and fertility. Szpakowska gives an example of recorded testimony to this kind of encounter during an episode of holy drunkenness associated with Hathor's festival. Such festival activities involved sacred intoxication, seen as a spiritual communion with the goddess. In such a state, an attendee might hope to experience the divine presence of Hathor.

Beer and wine were sacred to Hathor, so to experience divine adoration was to be enraptured and intoxicated. Divine drunkenness could soften the boundaries between the mortal and the divine and allow for the realms to overlap. The heart could fill up like a cup with the foaming beer of Hathor's love, nourishing the ka and ba. Drinking Hathor's beer in festival was thus a way of becoming one with the divine essence of the goddess.

From the stele of a New Kingdom man named Ipwy:

> *(It was) on the day that I saw goodness*
> *my heart was spending the day in festival thereof*

that I saw the Lady of the Two Lands in a dream
and she placed joy in my heart.
Then I was revitalized with her food
without that one would say, "Would that I had, would
  that we had!"
One is bathed and inebriated by the sight of her.[3]

Descriptions of this sort remind me a lot of my own lucid dreams. Frequently excluded from dream studies is the exploration of lucidity, ecstasy, and dream-induced orgasmic experiences. Dreaming is a multilayered, transformational state. The feelings that arise within a dream can linger for a considerable time upon awakening. Everyone is familiar with that awful gloom that pervades the day following a nightmare. An afterglow effect is similarly experienced following a divine dream. We shall explore these ideas further in later chapters, but I thought Ipwy summed it up quite nicely here.

DREAMS THAT DELIVER THE FUTURE

Dream interpretation was certainly a respected profession in ancient Egypt and considered an art and a science. Some dream diviners would dream on behalf of another person. In doing so, they intended to extract from the dream gods' instructions a cure, an omen, a course of correct action, or the identity of the perpetrator of a crime.[4] Many prognostic dream texts have been discovered that list common dreams and their meanings.

It is very useful to consider that unlike modern psychoanalysis, in which dream interpretation is almost exclusively concerned with unraveling the dreamer's inner world, their complexes, and childhood traumas, ancient Egyptian dream interpretation was overwhelmingly focused on discovering the future. I believe the nature of the ancient Egyptian language and writing to be of vital relevance in this respect— that the reason for the employment of literate scribes in the job of dream interpretation and the abundance of wordplay and puns in the prognostic texts lies in the concept of the divine, god-given nature of the ancient Egyptian linguistic system and script. The idea that the gods communicated through the visual language and sound values of the hieroglyphs means that literate scribes were most able to translate dream visions into coherent interpretations.

A good example of a dream interpretation text is the 19th Dynasty Papyrus Chester Beatty 3, known as the Dream Book. This papyrus was owned, but not originally penned, by the scribe Qenherkhepshef, who wrote a poem about the Battle of Kadesh on the other side of the papyrus. The papyrus was discovered in the artisan town of Deir el-Medina and is currently held (not on display) at the British Museum in London.[5] In this text, many dream scenarios are simplistically listed and classified in a fashion similar to a modern dream dictionary. Good, auspicious dreams are recorded in black ink, while bad, ominous dreams are indicated by red. Examples of auspicious dreams include eating donkey flesh, being given white bread, and burying an old man. Examples of bad dream omens include looking into a deep well, munching on a cucumber, and copulating with a wife during daylight. Most of these interpretations rely upon homophones and punning within the ancient Egyptian language. The unknown dream interpreter/scribe of the text further divides the (all male) dreamers into extra categories. There are those who are determined to be followers of the falcon-headed, righteous god Horus. These characters exemplify the beneficent, humble, and ideal type of male qualities in ancient Egyptian culture. And there are those who the text's author describes as being followers of Set, god of war, chaos, and storms. These men are immoderate, violent, and lusty redheads. Red was the color of Horus's enemy and murderous brother, Set. Set was also associated with reddish animals and the inhospitable and ferocious red desert. The dream interpretation would differ according to which category the dreamer was in. This identification of aggressive redheads likely reflects the spiritual connotation of the color red rather than bemoaning the behavior of ginger men in Egypt (although, as a side note, because of their Set-like complexion, redheaded people were perceived as having a kinship with the god). Some of the first records of the persecution of redheads came out of ancient Egypt, while redheaded men may even have been sacrificed to Osiris. Set dismembered Osiris in a violent and cunning attempt to steal the throne.[6]

Luigi Prada is another contemporary Egyptologist who specializes in ancient Egyptian dream texts and inscriptions. He makes the intriguing observation that a large part of a dream interpreter's skill involved analysis of the dreamer, whose status, sex, and other characteristics may have determined the way in which a given dream would be interpreted.[7] Depending on one's status and temperament, the same dream events could have different meanings. For example, if an unmarried woman dreamed she had sex with a snake, this would be considered auspicious and would indicate that she would soon meet a husband. However, should a married woman have the same dream, it would suggest infidelity.

The entries in Qenherkhepshef's Dream Book are generally no more than a couple of lines of hieratic, the priestly cursive form of hieroglyphs, used often for writing on papyri. The dreams described give good examples of the perceived law of opposites in dream logic. For example, dying violently in a dream is classified as good and somewhat cryptically means "living after his father." Whether this means reflecting the good qualities of his father in life or succeeding him in death is unclear. To be seen in a dream copulating with one's sister or mother was also considered auspicious and generally indicated a gain of some kind. Sex with wives and other women, however, was often considered a bad omen, and bestiality usually incurred a loss of property. Snakes are curiously associated with words, and many interpretations in the Dream Book reflect the punning and word-playing nature of dreaming.

To fully understand the many converging elements of these interpretations, it would be necessary to be very well versed in the language, script, material culture, and social conventions of ancient Egypt. Texts such as Qenherkhepshef's and similar tomes were produced all over Egypt and Mesopotamia, and wordplay is a significant and vital feature of all ancient dream interpretation. It continued to inform dream interpretation methodology and the stylistic presentation of interpretation into the later Greco-Roman period. Texts such as the Assyrian Dream Book and the Egyptian dream interpretation texts of the Ramesside age eventually came to influence dream diviners such as the third-century Roman soothsayer Artemidorus of Ephesus, who famously produced a five-volume work of dream interpretation titled *Oneirocritica* (Interpretation of Dreams). Artemidorus himself claims to have collated the information presented in his voluminous treatise as a result of many years of traveling in different countries and gathering oneiric insights, wisdom, and texts from a diverse array of diviners. The last section of *Oneirocritica* includes ninety-five dreams collected during his travels for his son, a wannabe dream interpreter himself, to practice on.

SLEEP PARALYSIS AND NIGHTMARES

In ancient Egypt, while it was seen that some dreams were a direct experience of divine-like gnosis, other dreams were puzzling, and these were the ones that required the skills of an interpreter. Not all dreams were benevolent of course, and nightmares could be sent from the vengeful dead. Sleep paralysis appears to have plagued the ancient Egyptian population and, as in Mesopotamia was considered to be the work of demons. To combat terrifying nightmares and sleep paralysis, ancient Egyptian people recited incantations. These scary experiences are described as "terrors that fall upon a man at night"[8] and recall common sleep paralysis phenomena and the succubus and incubus of mythological tradition.

A common household magical item that served the function of repelling nightmares was the defensive clay cobra, or uraeus, a representation of the sacred cobra that frequently appeared on the headdresses of rulers.[9] These were often crudely and quickly homemade. The small figures of cobras in a defensive, striking pose were placed around a person before they went to sleep, as they were thought to repel any evil entities that might wish to do a sleeper harm. The mouths of these clay cobras may have also served to hold a candle, a visual representation of the fire of their venom. There is also evidence to show that these cobras were carried, or repeatedly remade with locally found materials, over long distances by soldiers on military campaigns in the Levant.

It appears that nighttime was often considered something of a zone of vulnerability, a frightening abyss of malevolent darkness, a sinking into a world deprived of the good and divine light of Ra, god of the sun. Meanwhile, Khonsu, Iah, and Thoth, the gods of the moon, could offer some luminous protection while Ra was away. Khonsu was known as the traveler, the embracer, and the pathfinder. Along with Thoth, he helped mark time and was invoked as a supernatural healer. He was seen as especially adept at healing injuries caused by wild animals, and he guided those who had to travel by night.

Thoth was associated with temple sleep. He is recorded as having appeared on many occasions in dreams solicited by his famous worshipper (and by all accounts a prodigious prophetic dreamer), Hor of Sebennytos, originally a priest of Isis and later devoted to Thoth.[10] Hor had many divine-type dreams, and they appear to have come thick and fast, both solicited and unsolicited. Most of these dreams, recorded on ostraca deposited in the South Ibis Galleries at Saqqara, appear to have taken place in a variety of places within the animal necropoli. Hor served for five years at Thoth's temple at Pi-pefēr. Followers of Thoth often came to the temple with an assortment of mysterious and previously untreatable ailments, as the healing proficiency of an immortal god was regarded as eminently superior to that of a mere mortal quack. While in the employ of Thoth, evidence suggests that Hor dispensed the medical advice he gained in dreams from the Ibis-headed god to supplicants who visited the temple.

> *The house of rest (of) the Ibis, the day after spending*
> *   two days*
> *in making supplication, saying [. . .] before [. . .]*
> *"Come to me my lord Osorapis and Osormnevis:*
> *my great lord Osorapis, the great god, and the gods who*
> *   rest in the necropolis of the Sarapeum*
> *and the necropolis of Hepnēbes, together with those who*
> *   rest upon the sleeping-place/"shrine" of the House of*
> *   Thoth*
> *in Memphis: hear my voice my lord Osormnevis(?) and*
> *   the gods who rest in*

the necropolis of Djedit, together with those who rest (in)
the eastern desert of Heliopolis.[11]

DREAM REQUEST OF ḤOR—
TRANSLATED BY J. D. RAY

THE PROTECTIVE DEMON BES

Many magical objects and spells were employed by ancient Egyptian people to protect themselves from the negative forces of chaos while they slept. In particular, one of Egypt's favorite household deities, Bes, is often depicted on bedroom furniture and protective amulets, especially those made for children. Bes was a guardian of sleepers and a demon slayer, sharing some traits with the lion-bodied, sphinxlike god Tutu. You will notice that many ancient Egyptian beds are lion- or Tutu-footed. Tutu also specialized in protecting dreamers from nightmares and, in particular, any demons that had been sent by dangerous goddesses.

Bes is frequently depicted wielding a knife and is often shown alongside the fierce hippo goddess Tawaret on apotropaic hippo ivory wands. These wands were made to defend children and pregnant women and to offer protection around the perilous arena of childbirth. Bes is most often represented as a naked and fantastically well-endowed dwarf. He usually has a massively long unfurled tongue and a goblinlike face. Bes became a real favorite during the Greco-Roman period, and his wild, pugnacious energy was harnessed for apotropaic magic, the protective power that averts evil influences and malevolent entities. It was believed he could cheer up children with his clownish antics and simultaneously scare off ghouls with his grotesque grimacing and gargantuan genitals.

Some believe Bes to have traveled to Egypt as the demon Humbaba of Mesopotamia; others say that he emerged from sub-Saharan Africa. The demon Humbaba, who really is Bes's doppelgänger, is a mythological figure much like the Greek Medusa. He was decapitated by Gilgamesh in the *Epic of Gilgamesh,* and his severed head often served as a protective decoration on shields and objects of war.

Speculated by some to have been cult dream incubation chambers the so-called Bes Chambers were excavated by the British Egyptologist James Quibell at Saqqara in 1905.[12] The rooms are believed to have been built during the Ptolemaic period, but their true function remains mysterious. In Gil Renberg's incredibly thorough tome *Where Dreams May Come: Incubation Sanctuaries in the Greco-Roman World,* the author considers the suggestion that these chambers were dedicated, fertility-related dream incubation suites as unlikely. I imagine this idea initially gained traction because of the phallic nature of the decorations and objects discovered there, as well as Bes's known characteristics as a dream intermediary and to a lesser extent a fertility figure. Renberg first points out the lack of any similar Bes sites anywhere else, but perhaps more importantly he reminds us that Bes's monstrously massive member is generally acknowledged as serving an apotropaic function rather than a fertility-inducing one.

Renberg goes on to propose that these phallus-filled Bes Chambers might instead reflect the demon's incorporation into the Osirian and Dionysian worship that was prevalent in the area at the time. That being said, I don't think we can entirely rule out the possibility that the Bes Chambers had some sort of dream function, but perhaps, taking Renberg's lead, it was a function more intimately related to the cathartic, ecstasy-inducing Dionysian rituals.[13] Given the importance of the disembodied phallus in the Osirian Mysteries, this might make a neat match. The Greco-Egyptian god Serapis was also linked with the chthonic Osiris and shares a story of dismemberment with him. Serapis was incorporated into the divine Egyptian bull god Apis, too. In Roman times, Serapis often replaced Osiris as Isis's consort. It is known that dream incubation was also a feature of his sanctuaries, known as the Serapea.[14]

IMHOTEP, HIGH PRIEST OF THE SUN

There is only a small amount of contemporaneous material recovered from Egypt that tells us about Imhotep, a sage, architect, astrologer, and chief minister to the pharoah Djoser, the second king of Egypt's Third Dynasty (reigned 2630–2611 BCE). The site of his tomb remains mysterious. It is believed by many Egyptologists to be hidden somewhere in the vast necropolis at Saqqara, where he had a cult following.

The most famous evidence from Imhotep's lifetime is an inscription on the base of a statue of Djoser. The inscription lists the titles Imhotep held in the pharaoh's court, one of which was Greatest of Seers. His divine skills as physician seem to have come much later, when his syncretization with the Greek god of medicine, Asklepios, was cemented in Alexandrian Egypt. The popular identification of Imhotep as the architect of Djoser's step pyramid appears to derive from a single source, the somewhat enigmatic Egyptian priest and historian Manetho. Manetho's writings, the three-volume *Aegyptiaca,* are a voluminous history of ancient Egypt, thought to have been commissioned by Ptolemy II Philadelphus. This text was a major resource for early European scholars of Egyptian history and was especially influential in regard to the construction of a chronological time line for the ancient rulers and the division of dynasties.

Imhotep's influence peculiarly extends beyond his lifetime. His elevation to deity occurred about three thousand years after his death. From then on he became celebrated as a supreme and supernatural physician, a magician-scribe, and essentially a miracle-worker. In the New Kingdom (ca. 1550–1077 BCE), with his cult well established, his list of epithets increased to include Chief Scribe, Sage, High Priest, and Son of Ptah. His attributes also merged with those of Thoth, and his idealized image and character endures even into the Roman era, as evidenced by the inscriptions on a funerary stele belonging to the High Priest of Ptah in Memphis, Pasherenptah III.

I was a great man, rich in all riches, whereby I possessed a goodly harem. I lived forty-three years without any man-child being born to me. In which matter the majesty of this glorious god, Imhotep, the son of Ptah, was gracious unto me. A man-child was bestowed upon me, who was called Imhotep, and was surnamed Petubast. Ta-imhotepe, the daughter of the father of the god, the Prophet of Horus, the lord of Letopolis, Kha-hapi, was his mother.[15]

DREAM SANCTUARY

Imhotep shared a sanctuary with another deified architect, Amenhotep, at Deir el-Bahari.[16] This complex provides some of the best evidence of a dedicated incubatory site in ancient Egypt. It is well documented in various inscriptions, graffiti, and ostraca that therapeutic and oracular dreams were purposefully sought within its walls. Here, during the Ptolemaic period, even though Amenhotep appears to take precedence, Egyptian visitors petitioned Imhotep for divine dreams, and the Greeks called on their god of medicine, Asklepios, and his wife, Hygieia, goddess of health and cleanliness. Cleanliness is next to godliness, after all!

Amenhotep is referred to as the "good physician," while Imhotep/Asklepios is the "famous physician." Presumably, Amenhotep presided over other therapeutic treatments offered by the sanctuary, but dream healing was the domain of the famous one. It is believed that those who came seeking a cure at Imhotep and Asklepios's sanctuary initially wrote letters to the gods about their maladies. In this way, the temple attendants would have been able to tailor their treatments and provide relevant advice. Unlike visitors to the healing sanctuaries of Asklepios, it seems that those who came to Deir el-Bahari rarely received long-term care. Most patients seem to have come with minor ailments and left after a couple of days. It is believed the small barque shrine there was the chamber dedicated to dream incubation in the temple. A barque shrine was often the closest room to, or in some cases part of, the inner sanctum of a temple. Therefore it was considered a place of incredible divine power, one that the public would not usually be granted access to. This suggests that supplicants came to request a dream from the priests on their behalf. A barque was a sacred boat in which the gods traveled to the otherworld. Often these barques would be taken on ceremonial processions from one shrine to another during festivals, as they were considered divine housing for the living statues of the gods.

HIEROGLYPHS AND MAGIC

The entanglements of *heka,* Egyptian magic, and the divine manifesting power of the *mdw ntjr,* or hieroglyphs, are vital components of the dream culture of ancient Egypt. They help us understand Imhotep's role as magician, scribe, and divine physician. As was the case in Mesopotamia, magic and medicine were inextricable from each other in ancient Egypt. I suggest that the nature of the hieroglyphs encourages particularly bihemispheric thought processes; they provoke an expanded, constantly cross-referencing system of verbal and visual recognition. In fact, this language system is especially sympathetic to the way human memory works, by encoding, storing, and retrieving information. The study of hieroglyphs is therefore a natural primer for conscious dreaming.

Sometimes I think of the hieroglyphs as a holographic writing system, and I mean this in the spirit of the Greek meaning of the word *holographic;* that is, "whole writing." Within the nature of every single glyph there lies an echo of the entire system, such that each glyph really requires a holistic understanding of a living world of signs. The hieroglyphs depict the real things of the world. To be literate in ancient Egypt was not only to be able to decipher these signs and communicate in their spoken language but also to identify these same signs in the real world. You therefore might experience the world speaking coherently and directly to you. Certainly there would have been the opportunity for reality to present certain configurations of real-world images, which could be perceived and read as hieroglyphs. In this way, the world could speak to you. The divine could be said to communicate through the images of its creation—a form of ancient Egyptian dreaming, like that of the Aborigines of Australia.

It's no wonder that this language was considered sacred. A literary philosophy was factored into all features of ancient Egyptian architecture and design. Household and ritual artifacts and statuary often took the shape of a single hieroglyph, and the layout of objects within tombs and temples could, by this method, be made to spell out a protective charm. Arrangements like this can be considered living hieroglyphs, meaning that wall art, imagery, objects, architecture, and landscape can actually be read, as the visual language of the culture is fully integrated into its literary system.

To understand the consciousness of the time, we must try to understand that the hieroglyph is a magical thoughtform. They were used as a lexicon for manifestation. They have the power to imbue vital force and special qualities on a described person, animal, natural phenomenon, or object. Some of the signs might be considered sigil-like insofar as they can be used to invoke assistance from a god or other divine power. Many of the signs double as magical charms and were made into amulets to protect the wearer, to bring them good fortune and health.

The ancient Egyptian corpus of hieroglyphs is made up of different categories of signs that are phonetic, logographic, and pictorial. The language consists of phonetic glyphs that can be uniliteral (representing a single phoneme, such as b, k, and p), biliteral (signs that can be translated into two letters, such as mi, ak, and oo), or triliteral (as in the signs for was, wab, and nbw), as well as phonetic complements, determinatives, and pictograms, which are not sounded out. As in Arabic, ancient Egyptian vowel sounds are usually not written, so pronunciation of the ancient Egyptian has been surmised by knowledge of the evolution of its descendant language, Coptic. A single word in ancient Egyptian might contain a combination of several different types of hieroglyphs, and there are hundreds of known signs. Texts and inscriptions might be read from right to left or left to right; the correct direction is determined by the direction that the human and animal signs are facing. You read into the faces of the human and animal characters. Sign order also frequently shifts about a little to allow for an aesthetic harmony, especially in monumental inscriptions where a certain symmetry was necessary to attain the desired sense of harmony and proportion and satisfy the principle of Ma'at.

Ancient Egyptian language and hieroglyphs are truly fascinating to study. Even though I am still in the first few years of learning, this study has helped me enormously to get a greater feel for the ancient Egyptian magical and creative mind-set. This insight, apart from anything else, deeply transforms museum experiences. I am so delighted that the study of hieroglyphs has returned to the curriculum for children in Egypt. I think all children everywhere should learn about them, as they are incredible learning tools. There are also many other beautiful ancient hieroglyphic scripts from other ancient cultures, many of them still eluding decipherment.

Intuitively, I feel that the writing and language system of ancient Egypt is conducive to creating a feedback between the waking and dreaming states. Although hieroglyphs represent phonetic sound values and have a coherent spoken language attached to them, they cannot help but be deeply associative and personal, too. Images are always associated with ideas, in arrangements that are unique to the individual reader. This association process encourages and engages one in lateral and holistic thinking. The hieroglyphs grew out of a mythical and sacred landscape. They evolved from a preliterate artistic tradition of meaningful symbols and a reverence for natural forms and patterns.

If you consider our modern languages, with their abstract letter forms, it is clear that they illustrate a greater degree of separation from material reality. They sketch out the noosphere for us, that fuzzy mental layer of reality that cuts us off from the natural world. The Egyptian writing system, with its visual compositions, with its creative ability to turn the world into one full of readable signs, is the language of nature, and the language of nature is the language of the Divine.

The ancient Egyptian word for "dream" is *rswt,* with an accepted pronunciation of "resoot." The use of the open eye determinative to categorize the word suggests that dreaming was considered a visual phenomenon, that dreaming was the *seeing* of an other world.

DREAM MEDICINES AND SPELLS

A selection of medical papyri give recipes, formulae, and incantations for the purpose of beneficial dreams, sleep medicine, and the banishment of nightmares. The Egyptians had an expansive pharmacopeia and were known to have used poppy, wild lettuce, chamomile, lavender, vervain, frankincense, Egyptian henbane, belladonna, rue, cannabis, mandrake, and blue water lily. The alcohol content of wine was used to extract psychoactive alkaloids from plants. Many preparations were steeped in wine or beer for this reason. Such substances would have been used in incense, unguents, drink preparations, and as sacred food. Each medicinal plant had a spirit, a divine identity. Many of the compounds found in the plants that ancient Egyptians regularly used are very toxic and lethal in large amounts, so dosing was a careful and considered process acquired through experience and training. As was also the case in Mesopotamia, punishments could be doled out to those medical practitioners who overdosed and subsequently caused injury or death to their patients.

Nefertem, the son of creator god Ptah, was the god of perfume, and he was personified by the blue water lily, which was recognized as a solar symbol. A beauteous smell was seen to be a deific encounter. Poppies were believed to be made by the god Thoth. To be intoxicated on such substances, substances impossible to disentangle from the divine reality of the gods, was sacred and holy. To merely inhale the sweet fragrance of a fine flower was to be in communion with a god, to be lifted up and infused with their unique euphoric emanations.[17]

Many of ancient Egypt's most popular social lubricants are also aphrodisiacs: mandrake, blue water lily, and wild lettuce in particular. These substances would have had effects that could be felt in both waking and sleeping states, and they could provoke an erotic trance state. Arousal produces vivid dreams: as an aphrodisiac increases blood flow to erogenous zones, the likelihood of blissful and transcendent episodes of lucidity is increased, as expressed in this anonymous ancient Egyptian love lyric:

> *Your love has gone all through my body*
> *like honey in water,*
> *as a drug is mixed into spices,*
> *as water is mingled with wine.*
> *Oh that you would speed to see your sister*
> *like a charger on the battlefield, like a bull to his*
>   *pasture!*
> *For the heavens are sending us love like a flame*
>   *spreading through straw*
> *and desire like the swoop of the falcon!*
>   ANONYMOUS (C. 1085– 570 BCE)[18]

Initiatic Story: Amunet's Dream

The snakes devoured the frogs. In black, writhing knots of primordial mud and muscle, the frogs were turned and tumbled over. Helpless soft bodies with vast mouths agape, with bulging, glassy eyes frozen in awe. The frogs clumsily smeared their feeble webbed feet against the shining scales of the slick serpents, and the serpents encircled and swallowed them whole.

The frogs were in a terrible dream, invaded by serpentine sureness. The snakes were the living currents of the god Nun, the primeval waters. They were capable of containing chaos, each a tunneling maelstrom closing behind a wet, pink glottis. Swift, needle-sharp punctures, snake fangs, sank into the softest, fragile frog flesh. Delicate skeletons buckled as jaws came together to deliver an ecstatic injection of venom. There followed the extinction of each amphibian soul, the liquidation of their material assets. Evaporating ancient croaks were screams in some finer realm. The frog was a creature from a refracted time-world.

A moving mound of bodies piled up in the darkness. It produced the first lightless glimmer of life in the void. From this tangle of snakes and frogs rose the primordial mound, and from this primordial mound came consciousness. Threads of order and chaos weaved together upon the word of Thoth and created the beginning of time and the fabric of Sia, the female body of cosmic wisdom. The snakes and surviving frogs were the gods and goddesses of the void. These gods and goddesses became the patron deities of Khmunu. They formed the Ogdoad.

Thoth's discerning crescent moon–shaped Ibis beak fell on the primordial beings like a scythe. He made a well in the twisting nest, and together with the divine snakes and frogs, conceived the invisible cosmic egg.

Amunet, the first serpent goddess, split from the first frog god, Amun, and rose up to enfold the immaterial egg. As her abyss-born body coiled around the egg; she gave it form and made it manifest. From the invisible cosmic egg hatched Ra, god of the visible world, a bird of light. Ra is Creator of our world. Ra was mothered by the all-sexed and infinite Amunet, the mother who is father. Her hidden hiss from nowhere dispersed throughout creation. Amunet was the rememberer of the void. With newfound limbs, her body taking the shape of the first woman, her face retaining the features of a snake, she stepped up onto the Isle of Flames . . .

The priestess Amunet was receiving her tattoos. She was trying to remember the void of her namesake. She crossed her eyes in an attempt to escape the pain of the bronze needles scratching pigment into her skin. Two women, working in unison, marking at the same time, were creating a protective tattoo net over her belly to hold her future child in place. The pattern of their symmetrical afflictions created an imaginary sharp line through her navel. It felt as though a hot knife blade was pressed vertically into her flesh. The sharpness traveled up to the roots of her hair and down to the beds of her toenails. As the women worked, they sang the song of Amunet and the acacia tree, the Tree of Life.

Amunet could see this tree when she closed her eyes. The tree had fine, feathery leaves and was drenched in spikes of tiny, sweet-smelling sunburst blossoms. Its thorny branches held heavy seedpods, some green and plump, some open and contorted into desiccated curls by the dry heat. The tree's shady canopy was a refuge from the brilliant sun, a cool sanctuary for rose-gray laughing doves, for hoopoes the color of ripe peaches, and for bright green bee-eaters with gorgeous turquoise cheeks and black-barred eyes. The tree's rough bark was deeply creased like a long-baked riverbank. It split here and there, and where it did, it seeped beautiful amber baubles of aromatic sap.

Amunet's thoughts turned now to the gum from the acacia tree as she saw its smoke behind her head. She had mixed ash, smashed pellets of acacia resin, burned ibis feathers, copper, and vinegar to make the ink for her tattoos. In remembering her recipe and the arduous grinding it demanded, she forgot for a moment the monotony of her pain. It returned eloquently, and she winced. The needles had stopped.

Tonight she would sleep in Hathor's temple to request a dream of her future child from the goddess. This Amunet was high priestess of Hathor. Her belly was now wiped clean with beer, spread with honey, and wrapped carefully in polished linen . . .

Amunet came to the temple just as Ra set in the west. She came with her beloved, Nebwenenef, high priest of Amun. They were to lie in the sacred precinct of Hathor and receive the goddess's blessing for a child. They made the goddess offerings of foamy barley beer and gifts of sticky cone-shaped cakes made with chopped dates, crushed tiger nuts, honey, and spices. Nebwenenef brought reed baskets of wild lettuce and nuggets of turquoise in a gazelle-skin pouch. He had collected these pieces of the sky himself. Hathor was known as the foreign Mistress of Turquoise, and he had plucked these precious stones carefully from the veins of the earth at Mount Sinai. The couple brought armfuls of large, perfect blue water lilies, some open wide and showing their sun, some still in bud. The lilies' thick green stems were looped and knotted around the couple's wrists, moisture dripping from their freshly sliced ends. Amunet and Nebwenenef offered Hathor the golden, apple-scented fruits of love, the fruits of the mandrake.

Nebwenenef placed the heavy menat necklace of Hathor around Amunet's neck, and the priestess took up her goddess-handled sistrum. The rattle's metallic disks slid rhythmically up and down the long bodies of cupreous snakes. The percussive *sshshet, sshshet, sshshet* led Amunet as chantress to the statue of Hathor. She filled the mirror of Ra with beer and washed the feet of the goddess with it. Amunet cleaned Hathor's gentle, serene face and sensitive cow ears. Hathor's eyes were now filled with tears. Amunet decorated Hathor's head with a circlet of blue water lilies and mandrake fruits. The fresh, heady perfume of living water flowers and the sweet fruits of love mingled with the rich, atavistic fragrance of desert-dry frankincense, which bubbled in the brazier. From far away in time and place, the smoke of the ancestors sent its silky feelers about the inner sanctum of the temple. It disintegrated any lingering malevolent spirit forms and was soothing to the ka of Hathor.

The space could now be considered ritually pure. Amunet lifted the million beads of her menat necklace to be touched by the goddess. At her touch, this object was made sacred. Amunet opened her body to Hathor, raising her arms in adoration of her ka. She opened the gate to her heart, projecting her ka out to blend with the ka of Hathor.

Her heart, her ib, became intoxicated with Hathor's beauty. Her ib overflowed with joy, like a pot filled with foaming beer. She took this rapturous and devoted heart back to her lover.

Nebwenenef kissed the menat necklace as Amunet lifted it to his lips. He felt the faience beads rolling against his cheek; he tasted blue and green. Desire and joy rose up in him like a spring tide. His fingers traced Amunet's belly, passing over all the layers of material between him and her. He felt the net of fresh scars recently drawn upon her; tiny raised dots expanded with her breath. He was to place his seed within this net. Like a fish he would travel, silver and swift, through Amunet's rivers, to plant a seed within the holy water of her body. She contained Nun; she would encircle and nourish his seed. She would bring forth a healthy child.

He removed every layer of dress from her body—the fine creased linen, the dress of beads, her gold hoop earrings and snakey bracelets. Piece by piece, he revealed her. He poured oil and honey over Amunet's naked body and tore up endless plants of wild lettuce to make a bed for her. The leaves were oozing their milk as he lay Amunet on them. She was glistening like Nun and was as gentle and earthy as Hathor, with a heart as fiery and cosmic as Ra. Now they melted together, no longer in this world, in some fluid inner realm of ether. The firmament trembled as they held the stars . . .

A glowing, violet water lily was blossoming within Amunet, a radiant orb escaping from its unfolding bud. A warmth spread throughout her body, an exquisite fire rising up to her scalp. She felt the net of beads above her hips electrified. Pleasure absorbed her flesh and obliterated her mind. Her thinking was erased by the pure white light of the goddess. Deep within her cells, Hathor whispered. She knew she had caught the fish of Nebwenenef's first child. Amunet and Nebwenenef moved not a muscle all night, as if dead in each other's arms . . . the sleep of deepest creation. As they slept, the constellation of a new soul crystallized in the red night of Amunet's womb . . .

In Amunet's dream she was once again lying on her daybed receiving her tattoos, but now these lacerations were giving her the most divine sensations. Ecstasy rippled through her body with every application of bronze point. Each touch of bronze tip injected an elixir of ecstasy into the oceanic surface of her being.

She lay naked on the bed, her exposed sex swollen with an ambrosia of past and future achings. The two women who had been tattooing her were now tenderly stroking her between the legs. Her sex was developing like a consuming fire; it grew and expanded as the fire devoured her body. Her sex grew gasping, rising in the air above her. It became the body of a giant serpent, a legless lizard. Smooth and delicate skin covered its agile, muscular body. At its tip now developed a sensitive, pointed snake head. Then it morphed wet, jet eyes and flared its nostrils. It opened its moist pink mouth, and Amunet could see it was without fangs. Its mouth was gentle and craving, its forked tongue exquisite and delicate.

As the women lavished the serpent's body with more emphatic kisses and caresses, the serpent of Amunet's sex became enormous, primed for a rough lick from the holy cow of Hathor's tongue, which descended, drooling from above . . . Amunet's sex was now unrecognizable. It was towering not only over the women but also over the entire population of the village. It loomed over the gathered villagers. The gargantuan neck of Amunet's desire was bigger than her whole body. In fact, her body seemed to wither off and dangle at the side, like a deflated bladder or empty waterskin. The serpent of her sex roared into the sky. With this tremendous roar, which seemed to emanate from within a deeply buried reserve of personal power, Amunet came forth with the most ferocious deluge of milky semen, a brutal tidal wave. It rolled over and wiped out the world. This flood soaked the people of the village; it swamped palm roofs, rendered red mud bricks to mush, and turned paths to slurry. In the empty space behind the deluge, in her own groan of relief, Amunet heard the eternal hiss of the primordial Amunet. Inside her dream she remembered the void. She knew the void then. She knew the void as the source of the All. The All turned to silence . . .

When they woke at sunrise, the couple found themselves entangled in a den of sleepy desert boas—these creatures were the pets and protectors of the temple. Amunet felt jubilant and new. She stepped out of this pattern of vivid orange scales and living water hieroglyphs and up unto the dais. Gnosis.

Phase Five
Island Dreams
Minoa 3500 to 1450 BCE

In a dream I spoke with the Cyprus-born,
And said to her,
"Mother of beauty, mother of joy,
Why hast thou given to men
This thing called love, like the ache of a wound
In beauty's side,
To burn and throb and be quelled for an hour
And never wholly depart?"

And the daughter of Cyprus said to me,
"Child of the earth,
Behold, all things are born and attain,
But only as they desire.

"The sun that is strong, the gods that are wise,
The loving heart,
Deeds and knowledge and beauty and joy,
But before all else was desire."

XII Sappho

Audio track 5, "Bee," is the companion to this phase.

Minoa is perhaps my favorite ancient culture. Minoan Crete and Santorini were certainly some of the better places to be female in this time period, and on gorgeous, paradisiacal, fertile islands, too! Environmental archaeology reveals that in this era, Crete was sylvan and enjoyed more rainfall.[1] While native dream mysteries remain rather obscure, for me they are some of the most enjoyable to contemplate, especially as I am totally in love with the Greek islands. I think much can be gleaned about native Minoan religion from later traditions that transpired on Crete and other nearby islands.

There appears to be some continuity between the many Minoan peak sanctuaries used for religious rites and the healing complexes of Asklepios in Hellenic Greece. There is also an echo of the agrarian goddess cults of Crete in the Eleusinian Mysteries of the classical era 510–323 BCE. I suspect that much like the symbolic art language of ancient Egypt and Mesopotamia, Cretan art from the period is, to an extent, readable. It probably contains within it concise information about the Minoan spiritual world and, in particular, astral symbols.

It is certainly clear that goddess and nature worship were central to life on Crete as they were to those on many of the other islands in the Aegean and Mediterranean Seas. On islands from Samothrace, in the northern Balkan territory, through the cluster of the Cyclades to divine Cyprus, well nestled in the warm bosom of the Near East, the most ancient spiritual lineages of goddess and nature worship flourished for millennia. If you visit these islands today you will notice some of this ancient philosophy and knowledge preserved in the rich folk wisdom and tweaked Eastern Orthodoxy that make up much of their contemporary spiritual character.

We still have so much to learn about the enigmatic Minoan language. Linear A script, the primary script used to write the ancient Cretan language and perhaps other Aegean tongues, and beautiful hieroglyphs such as those displayed on the famous Phaistos Disc are still being deciphered. Many decipherments have been postulated—none entirely satisfying—but doubtless many more secrets will be revealed in the next few decades.

REIMAGINING OF MINOA

Sir Arthur Evans, the British archaeologist famous for excavating the large palace complex at Knossos, is also credited with applying the name Minoa to this culture—he named it after King Minos of Greek mythology. We do not know what the ancient people of the island called themselves, but the name Krete/Kreta undoubtedly originates with the some of the most ancient languages spoken on the island.

Evans was evidently quite a passionate, romantic, imaginative, obsessive, and detail-oriented man. His attention to detail can perhaps be explained by some of the peculiar habits of his short-sightedness. He is known to have refused to wear eyeglasses to see distances, and he walked with a cane he called Prodger, which that he used for exploring a colorful (if blurry) world. His close-up vision, on the other hand, is recorded as being excellent. It was noted, for example, that he could see fine details others missed. Perhaps this is why Evans seemed to relish tasks that required meticulous sorting and minute observation.

Evans's mother died when he was just six. In a letter to the woman who would become his new wife, Evans's father records a beautiful episode that nicely demonstrates his son's taste for the spiritual, romantic, metaphysical, and magical. He recalls his son burying a china doll in the garden. Its legs were broken, and the doll was buried with its personal effects and a butterfly. Young Arthur placed an inscription in the garden that read, "King Edward Sixth and the butterfly and there [*sic*] cloths and things."[2]

Arthur Evans also worked as a reporter, a head keeper at the Ashmolean Museum of Art and Archeology in Oxford (which is why the Ashmolean has the best Minoan collection outside of Crete), and even a spy of sorts during his lifetime. His political enmity toward the Ottoman oppression of the time most likely contributed to his somewhat Euro-skewed representation of the ancient culture of Crete to the rest of the world.

By the standards of today's archaeological discipline, Evans perhaps overenthusiastically reconstructed rooms at Knossos and moved artifacts around to suit his vision. He glued together and remade artifacts with zealous fervor and a good degree of poetic license. He commissioned frescoes to be freshened up, repainted, and even embellished. Much of this work was executed by his Swiss on-site artists and assistants, including the eminent Swiss archaeological artist Émile Gilliéron, Evans's chief restorer. Much of what Evans presented to the world was colored by his romantic enthusiasm to make the Minoans distinctly European. For example, the famous bare-breasted Snake Goddess of Minoa was a smallish, broken portion of a statuette when Evans initially discovered it. She had no head and one arm missing. Evans is known to have glued (perhaps not entirely belonging to the statuette) pieces together, and when no obviously related pieces were available he created new elements to fit his fancy and intuition.

Evans's excavations began in 1899. His findings and his dramatic journalistic flair in reporting them attracted a lot of interest around the world. In particular, his restored and reimagined figurines and frescoes launched a lucrative market for clever forgeries, which were made mostly on Crete. As a result, fake Minoan goddess figurines appear frequently as part of archaeological collections and museum displays. Such superfluous articles and Evans's romanticism have clouded perceptions of Minoan religious practice for a long time, and his vision remains embedded in our mental picture of Minoan iconography even today. Despite, and yet also because of this, the palace complex of Knossos is one of the most enigmatic and enjoyable ancient sites to visit in the world. To his credit, Evans took action to preserve the whole complex as a living museum by buying the land it was on. Other excavators might have attempted to shift the buildings and their elements into institutions around the globe. So at least Arthur Evans's creative and imaginative curatorship wonderfully preserved this amazing site and its finds in situ. His personal aesthetic tastes and discriminatory perspective, however, may have accidentally concealed and obscured much of what is probably astral and agrarian symbolism encoded in the ancient art and material culture of this immensely rich, intriguing island.

MINOAN PEAK SANCTUARIES

Crete's first human settlements are more than 130,000 years old.[3] It is known that Neolithic populations settled there as they migrated to Europe from Anatolia and the Levant, about 9,000 years ago. We expect that these early farmers already held animistic beliefs of the type suggested by the monumental art at sites like Göbekli Tepe and the ritual artifacts found in settlements such as Çatalhöyük. These beliefs were wonderfully articulated by the early people of Crete as they completely immersed themselves in the island's sacred landscape. Over time, these spiritual foundations became the basis of a magnificent high culture and a powerful maritime nation, one that meshed well with the surrounding cultures of Egypt, Anatolia, and elsewhere along the trade routes of the Near East.

The earliest ritual structures of Crete appear to be the peak sanctuaries, open-air ritual sites located high in the mountains of the island. Built alongside caves, they are likely candidates for dream rituals of some sort. Archaeological findings and votive offerings found at these sites suggest they were also places with a healing function.[4] The purpose of the peak sanctuaries overlaps with the use of caves as sacred sites of pilgrimage, and several caves continue to be regarded as the birthplace or hiding places of the gods, chiefly Zeus, but also Eileithyia, the goddess of childbirth. In many cultures, caves and mountains are considered sacred places, portals to an immortal realm, and they provide access points for humans to convene with the immortals. People would leave votives for the gods and goddesses and offerings to their ancestors in these caves, which were also often a source of good, sweet water, considered an expression of love from the Divine Mother to her children.

The peak sanctuary sites provide some of the earliest archaeological evidence for ritual activity in sacred surroundings. What appears to be of particular importance to the builders of these open-air structures is the view they commanded over the landscape and the opportunities they offered to witness the rising and setting sun and other celestial phenomenon. These sites appear to require only a moderately taxing pilgrimage for locals, so they were not usually at the very apex of a mountain. We might suppose, then, that they were intentionally designed so that the local coastal and agricultural people could ascend to the sacred sanctuary without major difficulties, and they could therefore be visited regularly.

Use of the peak sanctuaries gradually declined over time, when the palace system took over. During the palatial period, Minoans appear to have instituted a divine royal line, such that later ritual activities gravitated away from the earlier mountain divinities and focused on palace deities. *Palace,* in this context, was another term coined by Evans, one that probably obscures what really occurred in these complexes. Sites such as Knossos are ritual centers that at least in an earlier era maintained the peak sanctuaries as sort of satellite sites. Possibly there would have been a sacred pathway connecting the two places, on which festival processions would have taken place. According to Peatfield and Morris, the hierarchy of palaces may have had a religious structure, with priest-kings and high priestesses acting as intermediaries for the goddesses and gods and the people.

The evidence of clay figurines, called votives, found at many peak sanctuaries, indicates that these sites served a divine healing function. The votives discovered on Crete often appear to be small clay models of afflicted body parts. This is a very similar-looking system to that which is well recorded in the votive inscriptions and *iamata* (cure narratives) recorded at the later healing sanctuaries of Asklepios. In fact, the culture of placing votive plaques for healing and other purposes continues in the Greek Orthodox Church even today. The plaques are referred to as *tama* or *tamata* and are offered to the shrines and to the icons of saints in return for blessings and miracles. That this cure could still come in the form of a divine dream is further evidenced in the continuation of the practice in certain Greek churches, usually ones associated with a miraculous healing saint. This can be considered a continuation of the tradition of temple sleep and takes place often during festivals and pilgrimages such as the Dormition of the Panagia (Dormition of the Mother of God), which celebrates the "falling asleep"—that is, the painless death—

of the Virgin Mary, who is known as Panagia, "all holy," in Greek.[5] This feast day of the Orthodox Church occurs at sites associated with dream revelations and holy springs, such as the Panagia Evangelistria, a church on the tiny Cycladic island of Tinos.

SUN AND BULL WORSHIP

Like the Hatti and other cultures of Neolithic and Bronze Age Anatolia, the early inhabitants of Crete worshipped a solar goddess and a sacred bull god, representing Earth. Some believe the bull is the personification of the moon, but if this close symbolic relationship with the early Anatolian creation myths is plausible, the bull might represent a storm, rainfall, or an agricultural fertility deity. Beautiful murals depict young women and men participating in the extraordinarily athletic and daring ritual of leaping naked over enormous bulls. Perhaps it was these images that gave rise to the legend of King Minos demanding human sacrifice and the myth of the minotaur. Futhermore, in the mythological history of Crete, King Minos's wife, Pasiphaë, under Poseidon's enchantment, has lustful intercourse with the snow white Bull of Crete. She then gives birth to the Minotaur, whose true name is Asterius, meaning "Starry." Perhaps the sport of bull-leaping was a reenactment of the dance of the Earth and the Heavens, a form of sympathetic magic and psychodrama to ensure prosperity for the island and the people who depended on its continued abundance.

The "Horns of Consecration," another term coined by Arthur Evans, are a frequent motif throughout Minoan iconography, found all over ritual sites including the peak sanctuaries. Like the bull-leaping ritual, this symbol hints at shared roots with the creators of the Neolithic Anatolian cosmology. Some scholars have argued that the horns may depict not only those of a bull, but they might also signify twin peaks or the horizontal crescent of the moon as it appears over the horizon and the ecstatic stance of the goddess.[6] The Horns of Consecration are very similar to the Egyptian hieroglyph [◡, for *djw*,] meaning "mountain", which would make the symbol especially relevant to the peak sanctuaries.

ASTRAL AND AGRARIAN
GODDESS DEMETER

The central courts of the Minoan palaces at Knossos, Phaistos, and Malia are known to have been oriented toward the rising sun. Zakros and Petras in the east of Crete were oriented to capture the luminous rising moon.[7] There are similar celestial influences in the city planning and architectural practices of Hatti Land in Anatolia.[8] Similarly, in ancient Egypt, the Stretching of the Cord ceremony, under the auspices of the cosmic goddess and heavenly architect-scribe Sešat, determined the orientation, dimension, and proportions of temple structures. The ceremony would take place at night, when the site for a new building could be marked out on the earth with ropes and pegs, according to the heavenly guidelines from above, in particular in relation to the constellation Meskhetyu, "The Bull's Foreleg."[9] On Crete, the Minoans used a lunar calendar, and the heliacal rising of the binary star Spica seems to have been especially important, relating to their festival calendar and myths about chthonic deities and renewal.[10] Spica is the "ear of wheat" that the constellation Virgo holds in her hand and relates to the story of Demeter and Persephone. It is possible that the primary goddess of Minoa was already called Demeter by the Minoans (*Da-ma-te* in the later Linear B inscriptions of the Mycenaeans).[11] These Minoan festivals of death and regeneration are likely to have been the precursor of Mystery cults of the classical world, especially the Eleusinian Mysteries, which reenacted the kidnapping of Demeter's daughter, Persephone, by Hades, Lord of the Underworld, as well as the cult of Mithraism, which began with the adoration of the ancient Persian god of the sun, Mithra (who intriguingly also appears as a white bull). Over the centuries, the Mithraic Mysteries developed into something like an international old boys' club, a result of Roman military recruitment campaigns absorbing soldiers from conquered nations all over Eurasia as the Roman Empire expanded.

CHTHONIC AND CELESTIAL
ASPECTS IN RITUAL

The Minoan goddess put forth as the prototype of Demeter of the Eleusinian Mysteries, Da-ma-te, might be the poppy goddess, a distinctive female form found throughout Minoan material culture. This goddess may have had several aspects and manifestations and may have incorporated elements of Demeter and her daughter, Persephone.[12]

Ecstatic rituals that incorporated opium fumigation may have been used as ways to spiritually ascend or descend to the astral or chthonic realm. The later goddess Demeter, of the classical period, is often pictured with a cornucopia filled with wheat and poppies, although her poppies are more often the red field poppy, a common wildflower in wheat fields and often a symbol of death and rebirth, that perpetuates today when it is used as a symbol for fallen soldiers. Demeter is also frequently shown with serpents, as well as the dove. These two creatures respectively represent the chthonic and celestial aspects of the Minoan worldview. Opium from the opium poppy, *papaver somniferum,* was used to experience the divine in euphoric gatherings. The discovery of countless artifacts decorated with the opium poppy form—in particular clay poppy capsules that are shown to be slit, demonstrating knowledge about the method for gathering milky opium latex, or poppy tears. Opium poppies had been cultivated since at least the time of the Sumerians, who knew the flower as *hul gul,* "joy plant."[13] Also, small underground chambers with charcoal, opium residues and simple smoking apparatus were found with a statue of the poppy goddess at the Sanctuary of Gazi in Crete.[14] Poppies have been frequent motifs on countless ritual objects and containers, and these point to the importance of the poppy in the religious and ritual life of Minoan people.

Snake venom was sometimes used medicinally in ancient Greece, usually as an antidote for snakebite,[15] and it is has been suggested that a Minoan snake priestess or prophetess might have used the venom of snakes to achieve an altered state. Such a toxin might have produced prophetic visions and rambling oracular verse, but the many fake snake goddess replicas may have overemphasized the importance of the relationship between snakes and female ritual figures in Minoan religion. Minoa's Anatolian and Near Eastern influences and shared iconography should also to be taken into consideration.

Today there are several species of snakes on Crete; others no doubt became extinct over the years, which makes a snake goddess a difficult proposition to explore deeply. Some information may yet be uncovered as more Linear A texts are deciphered. Nowadays, out of all the species on the island, only the cat snake has venom, and it isn't usually dangerous to humans.

The Greeks have a folk legend that claims that oracular senses can be bestowed on humans when serpents lick clean their ears. This enables them to "hear" prophetic secrets, perhaps of the underworld, the domain of the snake. Many Greek myths explain that people can acquire "second hearing" and "second sight" if their ears or eyes are licked by a snake. This oracular and divine healing relationship with serpents may have later morphed into the many types of nonvenomous snakes that were employed in the dream-healing temples of Asklepios. The tradition carries into the present, in the snake-handling rituals incorporated in Greek Orthodox festivals, notably that of Panagia Fidoussa, the Virgin of the Snakes, which takes place every August in a small church in Markopoulo, a town on the island of Kefalonia.[16]

As in many magico-medical traditions of antiquity, both disease and cure were believed to originate from divine will. Just as you could be pierced with one of the disease-carrying arrows of Apollo, you might also be healed by the intervention of him or his son, Asklepios.

The snake, likewise, was a symbol of both poison and panacea. Small amounts of venom are known to have been used as medicine, and this power of the snake is reflected in the Greek root of the word *pharmacy,* which can refer to a healing or a harming herb. The pharmacy is intimately wrapped up in the arts of sorcery and neatly represented by the Bowl of Hygieia, one of the symbols used to this day to identify pharmacies.[17]

Initiatic Story: Bee Asleep

The procession wound its way through the gorge of the goddess. The tremulous air held by the ravine was medicine, potent with the warm, fragrant vapors of mountain herbs, of malotira, diktamo, thyme, wormwood, rock rose, rosemary, and marjoram. Styrax, cypress, and terebinth trees emanated an aura of raw incense. Clusters of daffodils, tall red lilies swaying in the breeze, and low-lying bursts of crocuses enjoyed the shade of the trees, adding the powdery perfume of their pollen to the atmosphere.

The people moved steadily over a rocky path. When they turned the next corner, a family of frightened kri-kri bolted vertically. The long ibex horns of the male agrimi clattered against low, dry brushwood and branches, and the animals' vertiginous ascent dislodged loose rocks from between exposed roots. White stones and chunks of dry mud tumbled down the rock face, falling silently toward the trickling stream at the bottom of the gorge. The people now walked in the shadow of the giant plane tree that stood before the sanctuary. In the lowest, thickest bough of the tree sat a brown honey buzzard in a regal white-speckled feather cape. The bird turned slowly to face the priestess at the head of the procession. He blinked for dramatic effect and then billowed up into the cloudless azure sky. Soaring, he threw a gray specter over the stone ramp ahead of them. After circling in a thermal for just a moment, the buzzard swooped down to a darkened ledge on the opposite side of the gorge and emerged from behind a large boulder, half a leopard viper in his beak.

The collected villagers looked to the priestess for her verdict on this omen. She continued observing the bird. The bird flew over their heads and straight, through the ocher columns of the sanctuary above them and flew purposefully into the ceremonial courtyard at its heart. Here the buzzard set the still-twisting head end of the leopard viper on the offering table and immediately departed.

This evidently was a good omen, for the priestess ushered them up the ramp. Finally they came into the stone coolness of the portico that surrounded the ritual stage. At the center of the stage was a wide, shallow bowl carved from translucent gypsum and filled with fresh water. The water was made holy and pure by the brilliant glare of the goddess. It became a solar mirror and cast divine light into the ritual arena.

The sanctuary had already been prepared by the Melissae, the holy bees, the pure priestesses who nourish with the gift of honey and sting with potent prophecy. The sanctuary was now bathed in a low fog of labdanum. The beautiful Melissae, having completed the ritual purification of the site at sunrise, were dressed in fine clothes and fancy adornments for the rites. They prostrated themselves at the filthy feet of the high priestess, and like the bees, for whom they were named, they began the intimate dance of the robing ceremony around the queen bee.

First they undressed the priestess. They peeled away her muddy garments and combed her hair. They washed her hair and body with sea sponges saturated in the sunned water of the holy fount. They rinsed her with vases full of herbal spring waters and made her breasts shine with poppyseed and orris oil. They brought her the immaculate layered skirt, its ruffled strips alternating saffron and indigo hues. Her bodice, stained a rich purple with murex, was laced and tightened. Her body was now wreathed in necklaces of golden bees and daisies and strings of polished shell, agate, and lapis lazuli beads. Her hair was braided with carnelian droplets and arranged in whorls and loops and pinned around her crown. Her hair was separated into small, oiled ringlets and laid against her forehead under a bright blue band of linen. The remaining sections of her long black hair were fingered into waves and placed gently about her shoulders. Her lips and nipples were painted with a paste of crushed black mulberries, beeswax, and olive oil.

Now the high priestess stood resplendent before her audience. She commanded those carrying the honey amphora and the two women with linen-wrapped infants to approach the offering table. These women placed small, faceless parcels that contained the bodies of dead babies onto the carved tabletop. The blood of the broken snake soaked into the edges of the wrappings. The vital spark of these children had been taken as a sacrament by the goddess while they were still in the wombs of their mothers. The priestess bound the babies and the portion of snake together with a wide linen strip. The fibers of the fabric had been soaked in the life-giving blood of the goddess, while the sacral knot provided a magical binding, binding the earth to the moon; it created a lunar analemma to fix a desire within the celestial realm. She invited the youngest of the Melissae to bring her a bowl filled with honey from the amphora, and she poured this slowly over the sacrificial parcel. She motioned for the oldest of the Melissae to bring her milk in the goddess pot. She trickled milk from the body of the goddess. The milk ribboned through the nipples of the pot's molded clay breasts. It soaked through the fabric, into the silent mouths of the infants.

The snake's blood marbled the honey. The mother's milk cast beads on it. The formula was sinking into all the crevices, activating the generative power of the inscriptions. It flowed along the table's gutters and finally dripped out of the channel that had been cut into the eastern face of the podium. It trickled onto the floor of the sanctuary, ran along the edges of the square floor stone, and sank into the foundational mud of the sanctum.

The youngest Melissae, with a blue-tinted scalp and sidelock, brought the priestess her labrys, the sacred double ax, the solar instrument of sacrifice and the tool for the reaping of the harvest. One could not exist without the other. Wielding it as a staff, the exulted woman touched the first blade to the north side and the second blade to the south side of the table. The arc of the sun slid along the uppermost curve of the labrys.

The hall for dreaming was laid out with sleeping mats. Terra-cotta opium burners were decorated with the face and ka of the poppy goddess. They released dream-making clouds, creating an atmosphere of fuzzy euphoria. The priestess closed the door of the chamber, and like babies drunk on mother's milk, the people of the village collectively fell into a deep dream.

Phase Six

Dream Panacea

Ancient Greece 500 to 530 BCE

Fanatics have their dreams, wherewith they weave
A paradise for a sect; the savage too
From forth the loftiest fashion of his sleep
Guesses at Heaven; pity these have not
Trac'd upon vellum or wild Indian leaf
The shadows of melodious utterance.
But bare of laurel they live, dream, and die;
For Poesy alone can tell her dreams,
With the fine spell of words alone can save
Imagination from the sable charm
And dumb enchantment. Who alive can say,
"Thou art no Poet may'st not tell thy dreams?"
Since every man whose soul is not a clod
Hath visions, and would speak, if he had loved
And been well-nurtured in his mother tongue.
Whether the dream now purpos'd to rehearse
Be poet's or fanatic's will be known
When this warm scribe my hand is in the grave.
      JOHN KEATS, FROM *THE FALL OF HYPERION: A DREAM*

Audio track 6, "Snake," is the companion to this phase.

The sanctuaries of Asklepios were often dedicated to both Asklepios and his father, Apollo. While the Sanctuary of Asklepios at Epidaurus is the most famous of these shrines, archaeological evidence exists for more than three hundred such sites. Asklepios was associated with the underworld. A chthonic demigod, he was a master of the healing arts, serpents, and canines, thought to have been born in either Trikka, in Thessaly, or Epidaurus, in the Peloponnese. His powerful Olympian father, Apollo, was associated with prophecy, healing, music, dance, and disease. He was often found cavorting with the Muses, playing his lyre and leading them in dance. Apollo later became associated with the sun and fused with the god Helios.

The mortal mother of Asklepios was Coronis, a Thassalian princess. When she slept with Apollo's enemy Ischys, Apollo murdered her, throwing her pregnant body on a funeral pyre. But in a fit of remorse, perhaps, he decided to rescue the child. He cut the infant out of her womb and delivered the baby, Asklepios, to the centaur Chiron, himself a healer. Chiron raised the child and taught Asklepios the art of medicine.

Asklepios is said to have been taught next-level divine healing secrets by a serpent in the forest after granting the creature a favor. In all of the many versions of this story he acquires his snake-entwined staff, the Rod of Asklepios, which in modern times is a symbol of medicine and healing. His prowess as healer eventually comes to rival that of the gods, and when he brought Hippolytus back from the dead, Zeus was furious. He promptly punished Asklepios by killing him with a thunderbolt. Apollo sought justice for his son, and when Zeus finally relented, Asklepios was lifted by Zeus into the heavens, where he was made a star in the constellation Ophiuchus, the Serpent Bearer.

As the adoration of Asklepios developed—perhaps initially out of some lengthy tradition of ancestor worship—great sanctuaries were erected all over the Hellenic world. In these centers of healing and supernatural dream cures, the people of the ancient world celebrated the divine healing powers of Asklepios. That these cures would often be fully actualized in a divine dream hints that something akin to a faith-healing event may have been occurring for some of the patients.

It was said that those about to give birth as well as those perceived to be properly at death's door were not allowed within the sacred precinct of Asklepios. In fact, there were often special buildings outside of the sanctuary boundaries where those about to die or give birth could go and peacefully perish or pop. Perhaps within the sanctuaries this would have allowed for an emphasis on issues that had at least an element of the psychosomatic.

Asklepios is certainly celebrated as a superb obstetrician. Issues of fertility, impotence, and granting wishes for a safe, healthy childbirth continued to be a priority at his shrines, as they were for his supernatural healer precursors. In the *iamatas,* the dream-healing cure narratives recorded at the temples, all manner of cures were attributed to the god, from recovered sight to healed limbs. We shall explore the nature of the cures offered at these sanctuaries in more detail later in this chapter.

The sanctuaries changed very gradually over the years, as a material and more familiar modern scientific method of medicine came to dominate Greek medical institutions. Yet the Hippocratic Oath (usually much revised) is a text still used in modern medical schools around the world. It requires a newly qualified doctor to swear by the old gods of Asklepios, Apollo, Hygieia, and Panacea.

For thousands of years it could be said that gods were considered the superior physicians. During this time it seems very likely that placebo, magic, and faith could have made up a significant portion of healing events, but then it's also worth remembering that most ailments are naturally resolved by the body over time anyway. Asklepios may have just been giving them a helping hand. All of the techniques employed by temple attendants and observed by patients are the sorts of practices that would help boost immune function and self-healing mechanisms.

Use of the sanctuaries persisted right into the Roman era. Archaeologists in 1964 discovered that the biblical Pool of Bethesda in Jerusalem, where Jesus performed healing miracles according the Gospel of John, was actually part of an Asklepion.[1] The sanctuaries eventually fell into disuse as a result the brutally violent antipagan campaigns of early Christian zealots, who sought to eradicate all forms of paganism, including pagan temples and sacred sites. The Roman emperor Theodosias I banned all activity at the Asklepions, but notably the Sanctuary of Asklepios at Epidaurus continued to be an important center for Christian healing miracles, Asklepios and Jesus being pretty much interchangeable as bearded, kind, son-of-God miracle-workers.

SACRED GROVES

There are several key features that can be found in most of the sanctuaries of Asklepios, beginning with the Sacred Grove. Trees were considered evidence of god-given life, and a healing sanctuary would often be surrounded by a sacrosanct arboretum. These trees were deemed holy and could not be cut down or used for mundane purposes, and severe punishments were levied on anyone who dared. This area was seen as one infused with nature spirits and divine power. The grove also functioned perhaps as a sort of spiritual buffer zone between the realm of mortals on one side and a sacred precinct of the gods on the other.

In the case of Asklepios, his groves were often made up of cypress trees. The cypress is a tree associated with the myth of Cyparissus, Apollo's *eromenos,* or passive adolescent male sexual partner. In Greek society of the time, a romanticized culture of pederasty marked initiatory transition from childhood to manhood. Eromenos were the passive object of an active older male partner, known as an *erastes.* The older man often furnished the boy with the gift of a wild animal or pet. Apollo is said to have given the boy Cyparissus a stag, which the boy tamed and loved very much. During a hunting outing, Cyparissus accidentally killed his pet with his javelin. The stag had been sleeping in the woods. Such was the boy's grief and mourning at the loss of his beloved pet that he transformed into a cypress tree, hence the cypress was often associated with death and mourning.

Trees have much older associated spiritual traditions, too, being a focal point of adoration in all sorts of animistic belief systems. They were frequently the symbol of a goddess, particularly the mother goddess Asherah, and they were often linked to solar cults, too. In Persian myth, the cypress tree was associated with honesty, freedom, and immortality. Ancient Persian legends tell of a time of famine, when people were forced to eat the cypress tree out of desperation, but when they did they became youthful and were granted eternal life. In the Orphic Mysteries, initiates were told the shining cypress would guide them through Hades. Cypress was also a favorite fumigant in many temples.

SNAKES AND DOGS

As is already well attested, snakes and dogs had by this point been recognized as healing creatures for millennia, and they retained their roles as attendant animals in Asklepios's temple sites throughout the ancient world. The snake and the dog were considered to be the animal forms of Asklepios. Snakes from the home sanctuary at Epidaurus would be taken abroad to identify new temple sites. It was said that the snakes would indicate when a site was deemed favorable by the god.

On a very practical level, snakes and dogs do offer good protection from vermin and are useful guardian animals. Dogs were allowed to roam around the temples and were no doubt used on occasion to lick wounds, as they were in the temples of Gula. Statues of the god Asklepios show him with his dog and snake. At Epidaurus there was an especially monumental statue of the god with his animal forms made from ivory panels, gold, and other precious metals and stones. Attendants were required to massage the statue with oil to prevent it from cracking, and it was said to have been built over a water hole— perhaps the chthonic portal of the god.

Snakes are obvious symbols of health. They have an ability to shed their skin and emerge young and new; they can hibernate and appear dormant during aestivation, the ancients may not have made a distinction between legless lizards, slow worms, or glass lizards, who otherwise look like snakes but are capable of regenerating their tails, unlike true snakes. Some snakes administer a potent poison that can also be used as medicine and venom antidote. The snakes employed at the temples of Asklepios were a type of nonvenomous tree snake that is still called the Aesculapian snake today, due to its long history of use in healing temples and its place in Greek mythology. These snakes grow to about two meters in length and are one of the largest species in Europe. They like to eat rats and other rodents, so they would have been useful allies at a temple full of offerings. They are also ordinarily forest dwellers, so perhaps they multiplied in the Sacred Grove that surrounded the sanctuary and received extra tribute there. The snakes were brought into the temple and were permitted to move freely around the complex.

As the animal form of Asklepios, the appearance of a snake in a dream was equated with the god himself. As such, a snake's touch was believed to provoke a spontaneous healing response in a patient. I have wondered whether there was a dream snakebite cure of sorts, whether the dream snake, as god, could deliver this panacea, with the idea of the dream being something of a mirror realm, an imaginal action required by the conscious mind to activate a bodily response. Certainly sleeping in a temple filled with snakes would likely guarantee seeing a snake in your dreams.

We know that during sleep, certain genes switch on that are not switched on during wakefulness.[2] These genes are involved in homeostasis, the hormone-balancing, cell-renewal, and detoxifying processes that occur in our bodies while we sleep. Healing and divine dreams are often lucid. What would be more likely than the appearance of a god to rouse an ancient dreamer from sleep's oblivion into lucid awareness? During episodes of lucidity there is a rare entanglement of the conscious and unconscious aspects of mind and body, and this self-healing mechanism is also uniquely activated. In this state, then, could we perhaps influence and direct our own self-healing mechanisms? For example, take the dream-induced orgasm. This provides evidence for the fact that the body can respond to dream stimuli. Could some endogenous healing response be mounted when we experience the full, conscious, and embodied effect of a supernatural healing event in a dream?

SACRED SPRINGS

Perhaps the most important geological feature of the typical sanctuary of Asklepios is the sacred spring. Clean, pure water was essential for the day-to-day functioning of a healing sanctuary. Cold-water bathing was one of the exercises in purity that the god demanded. In this, Asklepios could be seen to be something of an early advocate of the Wim Hof method!

There is always a chthonic element to springs, as Asklepios and his attendant creatures were of the underworld, so the spring was of special importance. Drinking and bathing enabled patients to become one with the chthonic element. To prepare oneself to enter the god's sacred precinct it was essential that you were ritually pure. Patients fasted, bathed, and dressed in white swaddling, as if they were babies. To pass through the sanctuary was in a sense to be reborn, and this neatly fits in with the temple's extra function as a vehicle for initiation.

HYGIEIA AND PANACEA

In some accounts Hygieia is the wife of Asklepios; in others, she is his daughter. Hygieia is the personification of health and cleanliness; her name is the root of our word *hygiene*. In fact, we have borrowed many terms from the sanctuaries of Asklepios. The *kliné* was the couch on which a temple patient would seek their healing dream, and from this word we get *clinic*. The *therapeutai* were the temple attendants and functionaries of the gods, and from them we have derived the terms *therapy* and *therapist*.

Among the Pythagoreans, the symbol of Hygieia was the pentagram, or five-pointed star. This was used as a mark to identify themselves to one another. But Hygieia's most recognized symbol is that of the Bowl of Hygieia. Many statues show the goddess holding and feeding snakes from a bowl or chalice. The symbol is still used to identify pharmacies in many countries.

Panacea was the daughter of Asklepios, a goddess of universal health. Her name has become synonymous with the idea of a cure-all remedy. As the primary and premier healing modality of the sanctuaries was the divine dream, we can see that Panacea personifies this idea of a universal cure, one that could manifest in a multitude of guises but was essentially effective in the same way for all ailments.

A divine dream offered the cure. This dream cure would be

procured by paying tribute to the gods and goddesses of the sanctuary. Some records describe patients as being invited by the god himself. In these cases he appeared in an unsolicited dream at home and encouraged the dreamer to pay him tribute and visit his sanctuary.

PURIFICATION AND OFFERINGS

Arriving at the sanctuary, it was necessary that you were already ritually purified. This usually entailed a moderate period of abstinence from sex, alcohol, and meat. It may also refer to not being too close to death or polluted by it. Once on-site, you would make your offerings at the altar of the gods.

Asklepios is said to have favored cocks, but being a generous and kindly god, he would accept any heartfelt token, even from the very poor. The very wealthy left fine gifts and funded exquisite architecture and decoration. They offered beautifully carved and inscribed votive plaques, statues, and objets d'art as thank-you offerings when a cure was successful, and in the hope of currying the god's favor in the future.

The temple attendants were assistants in comfort and health. They would care for the sick with healing food, assisted purging, prescribed fasting, exercise, herbs, and good hygiene practices. Catharsis was a vital part of treatment, and patients were encouraged to express themselves through art. The therapeutai would also set bones and perform certain surgeries. Opiates may have been employed for pain relief during these operations as well as to induce the best conditions for divine intervention. Temple attendants also worked as dream interpreters. Instructions for treatment were often delivered to temple officiates through dream encounters with Asklepios or by extracting coded information from the dreams of the patients.

The sanctuaries were not entirely dissimilar to a modern spa but with a decidedly religious and initiatory overtone. At Epidaurus, the sanctuary was incorporated into the Eleusinian Greater Mysteries with the Epidauria, a festival and procession that celebrated the healer's arrival in Athens and involved a great sacrifice and all-night feast.

Music, singing, and all the divine arts of the Muses were an important aspect of the healing environment. Many festivals and competitions were held at Epidaurus. There was a type of divine song called the "Paean," which was also one of Asklepios's epithets. This song was believed to call down the immortals from Heaven and petition them to heal the patients. There was and still is a vast and incredible amphitheater at Epidaurus, one that commands an outstanding view of the surrounding valleys and mountains. This structure is an extraordinary feat of ancient engineering and has marvelous acoustic qualities.

On-site at Epidaurus there was a circular building, a *tholos,* called the *thymele.* New excavations conducted by Vassilis Lamprinoudakis, professor emeritus of classical archaeology at the University of Athens, have revealed that this building was built on a much older structure, one that may have been made to provide a chthonic seat of the god in residence. That this newly discovered underground chamber represents the beginnings of an earlier incubation cult at the site is thought likely. This basement space may have been the earliest sleeping chambers for those seeking a dream cure and a dream audience with the god of healing.

As the popularity of Asklepios increased, large numbers of supplicants were moved into dormitories, with perhaps private rooms available for the elite. These sacred spaces were known as *abaton* and were reserved for incubatory practices. The incubation, or *enkoimesis,* was seen as a dream with special divine qualities provided by the sanctity of the sleeping space itself and its relationship to a supernatural entity. It may or may not have involved special dream-inducing potions. It might be the case that while the patients were under the influence of certain psychoactive substances, most likely opium, the temple attendants carried out certain dramas around them, acting out healing narratives as the gods—a form of hypnoidal psychodrama. Similar theatrical activities are known to have taken place at oracles and in Mystery cults.

In the dreams that came to them, patients were sometimes given riddle-like instructions for treatment. This could be interpreted and carried out by the therapeutai or even something the patients could do for themselves, but the highest and most direct cure was that of being visited by the god himself in a dream. Dream narratives and inscriptions (i.e., *iamata*) proclaim thousands of such successful cures.[3] In many of these narratives, Asklepios performs some sort of physically impossible operation on the patient, such as cutting off someone's head, emptying it of bees, and sewing it back on. Sometimes the mere touch of the god or one of his theriomorphic beasts is said to provoke a spontaneous and miraculous healing event. These accounts are numerous and were plastered all over areas of the sanctuary—a sort of early billboarding for medical efficacy. In and of themselves they would have had a powerful psychological influence. Certainly they could be seen as priming and reinforcing a placebo, hypnoidal, or faith-healing type of cure.

Remembrance and Lucid Dreaming

In some descriptions of the sanctuaries, the importance of the Titaness Mnemosyne, goddess of memory and mother of the Muses, is emphasized. The last ritual before incubation was sometimes an invocation of Mnemosyne accompanied by a fumigation of frankincense. Mnemosyne's role was essentially to allow the dreamer to remember their dream. If vital elements were lost through forgetfulness (her sister was Lethe, personification of forgetting), a cure might not be fully realized.

Remembrance in the dream state can be equated with lucidity. Being lucid means remembering who and where you are while you are in a dream. It's important to understand that the act of incubation as we have seen from Mesopotamian accounts is about lying down to dream, but not to completely fall asleep. It's about staying alert enough to detect the presence of a god. The particulars of this mode of liminal dreaming require a form of mental alertness and remembrance. The lucid dream may be induced during wakefulness, the goal being to keep the patient from slipping into the oblivion of deep sleep. It has been proposed that this may have been further achieved by some from of guided hypnagogic hypnosis or a dream-inducing potion. Perhaps temple attendants practiced hypnosis and autosuggestion. In doing so they might have enabled patients to stay aware as they were entering a dream, seeding those consciously unfolding dream worlds with healing intent and the presence of the divine entities.

Mnemosyne was psychopomp of the Orphic Mysteries. She presided over the recall of prophetic visions at the Oracle of Trophonius, too, one of four oracles associated with Apollo, located at a cave in present-day Livadeia in Boetia, Greece. As the mother of the Muses she gave birth to creativity and is thus the source of all that is divinely inspired. Through Mnemosyne, the divine spark of a human is fanned and fueled, kept active and alive.

Mnemosyne is thought to have named all things of the material realm. She is the goddess of eloquence, erudition, and sense-making and was invoked by the great poets and orators of the time when they needed to perform a passionate poem or give a rousing speech. She was called on to help dreamers vividly remember themselves in dreams.

I view Mnemosyne as the personification of consciousness. She represents a union of the celestial and material realms, the conscious and the unconscious. Through her heavenly connection she activates a divine spark in carnal reality. She inspires, she makes sense of the world and our experience, and she enables us to eruditely and eloquently live the story of our lives, knowing who we are. Mnemosyne offers us a reminder that we have a divine origin, that we still have the capacity to flow with the divine source of creation, to flow with her river of memory. Mnemosyne reminds us that our soul is immortal and divine.

In the Orphic Mysteries, Mnemosyne guides initiates into Hades, the Greek underworld. Here she reminds them not to drink from the spring of Lethe, even as it gushes so tantalizingly and refreshingly, and they are so horribly thirsty on account of being bone-dry and dead. She encourages initiates onward so that they might drink the water of Mnemosyne, or memory. When they drink of this water they are infused with the remembrance of their divine origin, and they recognize their true nature as immortal.

Instructions for the initiates of the Orphic Mysteries where etched onto thin strips of gold, rolled up like a scroll, and worn on necklaces. These gold tablets were like passports to Heaven, as their instructions read:

> This is the work of Memory, when you are about to die,
> down to the well-built house of Hades.

There is a spring at the right side,
and standing by it a white cypress.
Descending to it, the souls of the dead
refresh themselves.
Do not even go near this spring!
Ahead you will find from the Lake of Memory,
cold water pouring forth; there are guards before it.
They will ask you, with astute wisdom,
what you are seeking in the darkness of murky Hades.
Say, "I am a son of earth and starry sky,
I am parched with thirst and am dying;
but quickly grant me
cold water from the Lake of Memory to drink."
And they will announce you to the Chthonian King,
And they will grant you to drink from the Lake of Memory.
And you too, having drunk, will go along
the sacred road on which other
glorious initiates and *bacchoi* travel.[4]

The Oracle of Trophonius at Livadeia was known in the ancient Greek world as the Dark Oracle and was rather terrifying by all accounts. It seems to have only been sought out as a last resort, when no other prophetic wisdom was up to the task, and it was known as a veritable cave of nightmares.

First of all, it was required that you drank the water from the river of Lethe to forget everything you knew. Then you had to imbibe a cup of water from the river of Mnemosyne to vividly remember everything about the horrifying visions and nightmarish voices you were about to experience. The inquirer was then lowered head-first into a dark crevice filled with serpents and the cavernous sound of running water. Sometimes visitors seemed to have gotten bashed about the head. Honey cakes were taken to appease the snakes, and the experience was frightening and extremely discombobulating. After a thoroughly indeterminate period of time—could be days—the oracle seeker was pulled out of the hole and seated in the chair of Mnemosyne. In this chair they might babble incoherently or make some trembly utterances about the obscene visions they had recently experienced, and from this the oracle counselors could construct an oracle narrative.

Notably, when the Romans renamed and repurposed the Greek pantheon, Mnemosyne was absorbed into the Roman goddess Juno and later Moneta, the goddess of money. This is how we forgot about the goddess of divine memory and live now in a world of debt.

RESTORING THE BALANCE

The Asklepion cure was harmony and health. To bring about a healthy condition, it was necessary for the body to be harmonious. This is seen in the god's little pal Telesphoros, a cherubic sidekick he is often shown with in statues and reliefs. Telesphoros is the personification of convalescence, the bringer of fulfillment, of returning the sick to perfect and original health. This could be achieved in the sanctuaries through a purposefully curated environment of peace, calm, and purity. In such an environment, the human organism has the possibility to revert back to its original, perfect, unpolluted, birth-given design. The perfect environment acted as a mirror, one that could reflect back to the patients an ideal version of themselves.

Patients were lulled with heavenly music. They infused themselves with the nature spirits of the Sacred Grove. They bathed in pools and drank the healing waters of the sacred spring. Through these activities they absorbed the natural patterns of the Divine. They were subjected to this influence as long as they were in the residence of the gods. They were purified and blessed. They experienced a deep integration of body and soul. They received transpersonal therapy in the dream state. They were reborn.

ASTERIA AND BRIZO AT DELOS

Like Mnemosyne, Asteria was a Titaness. Her father, Coeus, was the personification of rational intelligence, and her mother, Phoebe, was a goddess of prophetic wisdom. Her mother was also the grandmother of Apollo and the moon goddess Artemis.

Asteria was the goddess of falling stars and nighttime prophecy. Nighttime prophecy refers to divination by the stars as well as by dream oracles. She was the mother of Hekate, a polymorphous goddess with a large number of gothic interests, including witchcraft, boundaries, magic, night, light, necromancy, ghosts, herbs, and poisonous plants. Hekate was seen as an underworld goddess and is frequently depicted with chthonic animals such as snakes, dogs, and polecats. She is often pictured holding torches and keys.

The holy island of Delos was considered to be the body of Asteria in Greek mythology. According to legend, this goddess was being pursued by the god Zeus. He chased her as an eagle, and to avoid being raped by him she transformed herself into a quail, and like a shooting star, plunged into the sea. As she hit the water, she turned into the Sicilian island of Ortygia (which means "quail") in the earliest records, but later she became associated with the Cycladic island of Delos. Today only a handful of people live on this tiny island. All are employees of the Greek Ministry of Culture, and the group is made of up largely of archaeologists, conservators, craftspeople, and surveyors. Delos is one of the most important mythological sites of the ancient world, and the excavations there are among the most extensive in the Mediterranean. It was considered a sacred sanctuary even in antiquity, as it later provided sanctuary for Asteria's sister Leto to give birth to Apollo and Artemis.

Gil Renberg believes there is good evidence of an oracular shrine existing on Delos, one dedicated to a dream prophetess named Brizo. Brizo's name is thought to come from the Greek verb for "to slumber," and she seems to have been particularly concerned with protecting the island's maritime population. It is unknown whether she had any connection to the goddess Asteria, but given the setting of the shrine it is not unlikely that there was some form of continuity in the oracular traditions. Brizo was said to be a favorite of mariners' wives, who took offerings to her shrine in exchange for her blessing on seagoing vessels. The wives made sacrifices in exchange for the protection of sailors and fishermen. As well, Brizo may have been the woman to consult if a person was lost at sea.

DIVINATORY INCUBATION
OF AMPHIARAOS

Amphiaraos, or Amphiariaus, was also associated with Asklepios and the healing-dream arts, as well as being a legendary seer and chthonic demigod of Greek mythology. The practice at Amphiaraos's sanctuaries seems to have been primarily concerned with prophetic revelations but increasingly took on healing functions when the plague hit local populations. His sanctuaries shared many common features with those of Asklepios, including a Sacred Grove and sacred spring, into which visitors would throw coins as payment to the god when they had a good result. It had a temple and baths, too. In the temples of Amphiaraos, he often borrowed the children of Asklepios to bolster his divine authority. There was frequently a theater and other ritual buildings.

From the second-century CE Greek travel writer and geographer Pausanius:

> I think that Amphiaraos most of all dedicated himself to interpreting dreams. It is clear that when he was considered a god, he set up an oracle of dreams. And the first thing is to purify oneself when someone comes to consult Amphiaraos, and the purification ritual is to sacrifice to the god, and people sacrifice to him and to all those whose names are on (the altar), and when these things are finished, they sacrifice a ram and spread out its skin under themselves, lie down waiting for the revelation of a dream.[5]

When prophetic dreams were desired, it seems to have been a custom across the Hellenic world to sacrifice a black ram and lie on its hide.

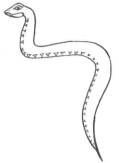

Initiatic Story: The Pool of Mnemosyne

Made drowsy by a fumigation of frankincense in this tiny chamber, my memories are forming and reforming in the smoke. They are being colored and reimagined by the cosmos within me. This is how memories are made—like the smoke of a galaxy in the mind, curling and breaking up, gathering in the recesses . . . Occasionally this smoke takes up the golden glimmer of divine remembrance. Sometimes it reels from the blinding lightning bolt of inspiration. Now it is settling into the darkest corners of my mind's labyrinth, barely rousable. The smoke of the soul falls in the same patterns. It keeps reentering the same atmospheres over and over. Over time, the smoke of the spirit learns to hold onto form . . .

Asklepios stands naked in a curved niche, holding his serpent-entwined staff in his hand. His beauteously white marble visage is mobile in the light of the oil lamps. The snake inches up his staff to share the healing, tranquil breath of the god, to lick clean the man's ears, so that the mortal fragment of him might hear his divine secrets again.

Buoyed up on the colorful memories of frankincense, I notice the person who brought me here. He is standing in the doorway. I can see a totality in the face of my keeper. I share his memories. In the matrix of his face I can see every experience of his life encoded. I know his sufferings and his triumphs. Intuitive memory comes to me from the goddess Mnemosyne, and he sings her hymn to me. And as I remember you, dear Mnemosyne, you are remembering me, and you are recovering my soul.

You whisper to me about all the loving, healing ways of Asklepios. Your words bring the marble muscles of my god to life, and I can feel him stroking my brow with his cool fingertips. The waking part of me subsides into sleep . . . In this dream I am guarded from oblivion by your wisps of remembrance. I am in the house I grew up in as a child. I am standing in the space between the rooms on the upper level. Through a window I can see a courtyard down below, and in this courtyard there is a layer of snow and a giant lizard being taken to its execution. The two men holding the lizard cut the creature's thick throat with a knife. I see that three droplets of red blood are left in the white snow.

Now I wake up—within the dream—for three days, and every day I wake up to discover a linen sheet bloodied with sacrificial lizard juice. It is placed at the end of my bed by a stranger. I wear a golden star on my breast, and this permits me to hear harmonies. In the courtyard now there is a rectangular stone pool, and it is filled with salamanders. They all have yellow, fiery bellies. They are swirling around and around . . . the water is sloshing about, and the snow has melted.

I am walking next to a maze and I see a spotted dog. The man with the dog is pouring oil all over it. He thinks he will set the dog on fire. I do not want to hear the dog scream, so I run into the maze. Inside the maze, when I am parallel to the man and his dog, I look into the hedge. There is a tiny, infinitesimally small, transparent egg. This egg has been laid by an ancient insect-size bird that flashes like a jewel. The bird has invisible wings and a long beak like a sword. As I observe this egg, I feel a wave of bliss roll through me, as if the crystal capsule of some exotic elixir has broken open inside my heart. Then I am back in the dream chamber, only now the ceiling is gone and I am very small. Asklepios is vast, and he dwells in the pure white clouds above me.

My god floats down to me from the sky. He is pure golden light, and he loves me so much. He extends his fingertips toward me. My body is exploding with yearning and delight at the anticipation of his touch. He walks down from Heaven and steps directly into my body, even the tiniest parts of me . . . I can feel them and see them. They are all bunched up and twisted like dry carob pods. These pods unspiral and become like a foothold for my god. With each footstep he takes into me, a rung lights up like a radiant ladder. Each touch of his lighted step, every dazzling footfall, makes me more and more whole. I am full of Heaven and being mended. Asklepios resounds in me, he weaves me back together, and I know of this because you, Mnemosyne, you guide me in the dream realm.

Asklepios gently takes my body back to its divine design. I feel as though I am being perfected by this theater of my psyche. His touch can recalibrate my matter and soul. His healing light irradiates my poor blood. It speaks in a divine, wordless language to the deepest part of me. It burns off everything that is not good and pure. And still you are holding my hand, beloved Mnemosyne!

You now take me into a dark, radiant underworld. A river of night flows into the black sun of forgetting, the sun of Lethe, your sister. Lethe is trying to wash out my memory in this mirror-world of dreams, but I hear your voice. In spiraling golden jets, your voice flows out to me. From the halo around Lethe's abysmal, empty face come the memories of past and future lives. They reverberate with your voice, they travel along the plucked strings of Apollo's lyre. Those are the same strings that carried my paean to the gods to you.

You are standing in gleaming robes, cloth spun with the golden silk of a million spiders' webs. You stand in all your heavenly power next to the bright cypress tree that glows like a moon in the gloom of Hades, and I say:

I am the child of Earth and starry Heaven. I am parched with thirst and I perish, but give me quickly refreshing water to drink from the Pool of Mnemosyne so that I may take my place among the other initiates.

You lift a cup to my lips, and I drink the soul of your water . . . drinking from the Pool of Mnemosyne . . .

Dreams of the Future

Starting . . . Now

*I found myself in a great futuristic city at night, with
beautiful architecture and dazzling lights. I became lucid
and remembered my experiment. As I looked around at
the awe-inspiring scenery, I shouted as loudly as I could,
"This is amazing, this is amazing!" I could feel my voice
box moving slightly and with effort. I felt a deep wave of
joy roll through my body.*

SJ VOICE BOX DREAM EXPERIMENT

We know that dreams have played an absolutely vital part in the
development of human culture and even the evolution of human
perception and consciousness. It has been my aim in this book to bring
some of the lesser-known aspects of this rich and fascinating dimension
of inner life to light, even though I have presented only a fraction of the
cultural legacy of dreaming. What I really hope to do is to encourage
you to explore the dream state personally and ask philosophical
questions about what *the dream* can reveal about the rest of your life.

What of our dreams now? I think dreams are in danger, and that
has been the best inspiration for me to write this book. If dreams are

Audio track 7, "Sacred Grove," is the companion to this phase.

in peril, then so, too, is our health, on an individual and a collective level. Digital dementia is a very real problem, one that is shown to affect cognitive abilities, to blunt memory, and to wither our emotional-processing faculties.

When we surrender our consciousness to technology, to more and more inane, mindless, disengaging distractions, we lose our powers of memory. Our subtle dream worlds are easily swathed in brain fog. If we wake up in the morning and habitually reach for our devices, this inevitably entrains us to the idea that *they* are the thing we have to do, to look at, that their world is the place where we need to mentally be. In this respect I can see a parallel with the effect that home-building had on the perception of our ancestors, we are expanding and projecting an image of ourself into an imaginal space. The digital home does not really exist, unlike the constructions of our ancestors, so our attempts to live in it are bound to cause disassociation and anxiety. There is no axis mundi that anchors us to the internet.

On a more pragmatic note, we are also simply going to bed later and later, as artificial lights reconfigure their luminous projection routes through our brains and eyes.[1] In many instances we are not getting even the bare minimum of sleep that's necessary for ordinary, healthy biological functioning.[2]

Through our devices, even the physical way we *look* at the world has changed. A new mode of seeing, determined in many cases by the habitual use of social media and screens, significantly affects the way we process stress, anxiety, and trauma in our waking life as well as in our dreams.[3] Our predominate daily eye movements have shifted from left-to-right movements that scan the depth of field of a natural, real-life environment, to close-range, rapid, up-and-down movements associated with looking at a screen and scrolling on handheld devices. Such eye movements are known to actively encourage and promote anxiety and panic. A technique known as Eye Movement Desensitization and Reprocessing (EMDR) is an effective trauma therapy that provides evidence for how eye movements influence emotional memory processing.[4]

We are now a culture unhealthily addicted to technology, to artificial light and constant communication. That some children begin to feel sick and anxious when they have their phones taken away; that people are reading, loving, moving, drawing, singing, and dancing less; that most of our contact with other people is through a keypad or box on a screen is enormously devastating.

If we wish to preserve our dreams, we need to completely invest in a lifestyle and philosophy that is conducive to producing wonderful dreams. We need to cultivate a culture of dreaming that celebrates this very special and personal part of being human.

New technologies could be very useful in dream entrainment. For example, virtual reality could be harnessed to encourage lucid dream awareness. In the VR realm you are ostensibly, sensorily participating in a full-body experience of an imaginal three-dimensional reality rather than just passively observing a screen. However, without a spiritual framework, that which is so special about dreaming can still escape us. Conscious dreaming is part of a spiritual reality. It can be a tool for the psyche to integrate experience, a methodology to become the best version of ourselves that we can be. In our dreams we might see an exaggeratedly excellent or extremely pathetic version of ourselves. Sometimes we see our worst qualities highlighted, or the deluded, wishful thinking of an inflated ego. Dreaming is most useful when it presents us to ourselves as we truly are. And we can know we are emotionally evolving when we see that true and honest version of ourselves becoming thoroughly loveable.

DREAM MEMORY AND LUCID DREAMING

For me, a lucid dream is simply a dream in which I remember who and where I am. In this process of remembering I am often able to control my environment or manifest people, places, and things. But control is really the lesser part of the experience. The best is the feeling of ecstasy and delight that comes with being utterly present, aware, and free in a uniquely creative and imaginal realm. Freedom makes up the biggest part of this bliss. I am convinced that this dream ecstasy has healing potential, that it is the essence of the ancient divine dream experiences I have explored in this book.

We should learn more about the wisdom of ancient dream sanctuaries. Dreaming should be incorporated into modern therapeutic treatments, and sleep hygiene should be of extra importance in hospitals and treatment centers. Much in the same way psychedelics have their place in integrative therapy, so, too, does dreaming. Dreaming is also a practice that can done at home and continued for the rest of your life, without any cost, detrimental consequences, or risks of dependence.

Dream memory is weird. In the dream state it can be as though you have access to a whole other class of memory. Even the memories of distant past dreams can be cross-referenced and referred to and can sometimes be rerun at will. Time appears to function differently in this parallel realm. Sometimes the sense of memory is overwhelming, like a tidal wave of past, future, and current dream lives. There can be profound sensations of déjà vu. When we remember our dreams, we go through a process of remembering ourselves. When we know our dreams, our dreams seem to know us better.

Many people have nightmares because they are not honest with themselves and/or other people when they are awake. In such cases, dreams bubble up from the unconscious, because that is where the true nature of a person lies. When the ego releases control in sleep, the unconscious rises to the surface and manifests as nightmares, violent dreams, shame, anxiety, and guilt. If people have unpleasant dreams or night terrors, they often choose to suppress them by using alcohol, cannabis, or prescription medications. Antidepressants are well known for reducing the duration and quality of REM sleep cycles. But if we do not face our dreams, we can end up stuck in a psychological rut, as we are not processing or integrating our experiences and trauma. We must face and integrate the shadows lurking in our dreams if we want to grow.

THE MEMORY PALACE

The memory palace technique, or method of loci, is a mnemonic device people use to remember vast amounts of data. Pieces of information are attributed to features of an imaginal, architectural, and landscaped environment. When you want to recover information, you take a mental journey though this mind map. Like a dream, our memory palace is created as our personalities and psyches evolve and develop over time. As babies we spend the largest portion of the day in dreaming sleep, building our impressions of the outside into a private inner world, one that is constantly added to and revised throughout our lifetimes.

I am sure I can remember dreams from the time I was an infant. In these dreams there are hardly any features, just something like a white room. As I grew up, these dream spaces were filled in with features— first furniture, animals, people, and architecture; and then great, expansive vistas; and eventually whole foreign countries with large populations and exotic birdlife.

Often in dreams we return to our childhood home or some amalgamation or reconfiguration of it. As children we can remember incredible details, and this helps make the remembered features from our childhood extra vivid in dreams. Many people have recurring dreams of being at school. It is very worthwhile to explore the idea of how old the dream version of yourself is. Are you seeing a younger version of yourself? Are you stuck at a certain stage of development? Are you realistic about who you really are? Are you wishing your life away?

As a child I started the habit of dream mapping. I have always been keen on maps of imaginal and make-believe worlds, and I loved Narnia and Alice in Wonderland and all those stories about dreams and neverlands. These maps fed into my dreams. My dream world was a place I visited every night; it had landmark features, dream people, birds, animals, zoos, shops, a school, houses, rivers, oceans, trains, and stations. I might arrive in a different location of the dream world every night, but I knew where I was in relation to my map. In making my map, I realized I was making a feedback system between dreaming and reality. The more I worked on my map, on the conscious constructions of my dream world in my real world, the more deep and detailed my dreams of exploring that map's landscape became.

DREAM LIGHT

Light from the world produces a negative impression when we close our eyes, a dark radiance. The powers of imagination and memory fill in gaps, reconfiguring and conjuring seeable phenomena in an attempt to interpret or visually articulate the subtle sensory signals of our dark inner world. The light quality in dreams is a beautiful thing to contemplate. Light seems to emanate from the things of the dream world rather than from an outside source, and colors are different. We see so much in our lifetimes, we could not possibly fully comprehend everything we see or we would be swamped with information. But what we choose to see should be considered as dream food.

Frequently at my workshops people tell me they have lots of nightmares, and usually the first question I ask is if they watch horror films, which they often do. Horror films are, I'm afraid, a terrible diet that disquiets the mind. Some supersymbolic and graphic archetypal films like the psychomagic *Holy Mountain* of Alejandro Jodorowsky can work brilliantly, though. Jodorowsky is my favorite dream film director. *Holy Mountain* is a perfect example of how art can be used as a tool to activate personal transformation. Like the ritual psychodramas of the Mystery cults in the ancient world, we can live through myths and archetypes and integrate them into the narratives of our dreams. Narrative, tarot, and other divinatory systems like runes and astrology can also help us configure ourselves into the fabric of a mythic reality.

Dreams are magnets for symbols and signs. They seem to use everything they have at their disposal; all the images, experiences, and emotions we have gathered consciously and unconsciously in waking life allow us to transmit and integrate subconscious thoughts, feelings, and memories into our conscious awareness. Who can say whether dreaming is not also a mode in which we can connect to some sort of greater mycelial mind, one beyond the perceived limits of our individual human bodies?

Many proficient lucid dreamers had nightmares as children. Lucidity seems to develop at times as a sort of safety mechanism of consciousness, to enable the dreamer to wake up when a dream becomes scary. If children and adults learn to instead wake up within the dream itself and confront or challenge their dream fears there, the shadows can integrate. As the sense of power shifts from shadow to conscious awareness, there is an inner alchemical process that occurs. Often such nightmares, especially if they are of a recurring nature, will not appear again.

As a child I had a recurring nightmare theme of being chased. In one of the dreams I was being pursued by a group of bloodthirsty transformers. Somehow in this dream I knew I had found an extraordinarily good hiding spot, a supernaturally safe place—it was under the tarpaulin of a boat. In the strange dreaming logic of my mind, I knew that no one apart from me knew of this hiding spot. So when I was eventually discovered by the transformers, I had a dream epiphany. It revealed to me that these transformers were *me!* My fear of them completely evaporated. In the dream, their faces melted with my revelation, but more importantly, I never had the chasing nightmares again.

Personal mythology is a transpersonal psychology approach to dreaming that was conceived and described by psychologists Stanley Krippner, Dennis Granger, and David Feinstein.[5] In the personal mythology method we explore the recurring motifs and themes of our dreams throughout our history. This might involve poring over old dream diary entries, artwork and ideas, dream perceptions of self, and reflections on dream relationships. The goal is to identify the roots and origins of our particular dream symbols, narrative idiosyncrasies, preoccupations, totem figures, scenery, and archetypes, tracing their ongoing evolution from childhood into adulthood and creating our own psychodramatic rituals to release childhood trauma, depression, and other neurotic complexes that diminish our joy. We learn to recognize these motifs consciously and highlight them in the dream state, and this can increase the chances of becoming lucid. As our awareness of dream content deepens, our most recognizable symbols and motifs can become triggers for lucidity.

Visual memory games and engaging in the practice of active recollection when awake can be an effective way to enhance our imaginal abilities. Techniques could include visual reimagining of already dreamed dreams, turning dreams into stories, word and memory boardgames, world-building play, guided meditation journeys, divination and magic, creating art, remembering real-life adventures and experiences, looking at old photos, and daydreaming and fantasizing. Mental exercises such as these help us enormously in developing our powers of imagination. Reading novels, watching symbolically rich and visually impactful movies, writing diaries and stories, drawing, and seeing things of awe-inspiring beauty are all very effective tools for enhancing the powers of the imagination.

Dream Speech and Dream Recording

A common feature of nightmares is that of crying out in fear or screaming for help, but no sound comes out. You can feel the physical effort going into your anguished wail, but there is silence or else a squeak, or perhaps just a weak and feeble whisper. This is because your voice box is actually actively making the micro-movements of a scream while you are dreaming. The same applies when you speak words in dreams. Scientist and dream researcher Daniel Oldis and his team have been attempting to decode what we say in dreams by translating these silent, laryngeal micro-movements into readable vocal patterns.[6] Other researchers are conducting experiments that attempt to create in-dream, two-way communication with the dreamer by sending aural cues to a subject in REM sleep and then asking the subject questions when they are inside a dream. These questions are frequently incorporated by the dreamer into the reality of the dream, so they may come from a dream character, the TV, or the radio.[7] While still in a lucid dream, the subject is able to answer these simple questions by using a set of pre-agreed-on eye movements. Upon awakening, the dreamer is then often able to recall the questions. The nature of this kind of conscious communication from inside a dream is very likely to significantly influence the content of the dream itself. Our dreams manifest through sensory input, thoughts, ideas, and words.

This kind of work is a continuation and evolution of the research carried out by people like Keith Hearne and Stephen LaBerge, who first conducted sleep lab research in the 1970s and '80s in an attempt to demonstrate that lucid dreaming is a unique state of consciousness in which a dreamer is self-aware and, when especially skilled, able to communicate this fact to scientific observers using ocular signaling.[8]

Eye muscles are among the few structures of the body not significantly affected by the muscular atonia that disables us during sleep and prevents us from acting out in our dreams.[9] Researchers had successful results in activating lucidity after developing simple technological devices that could send sensory signals to a sleeper once REM sleep had been detected. Hearne's invention was the Dream Machine, which upon REM detection sends an electrical pulse to the median nerve at the wrist; LaBerge's was the NovaDreamer, an eye mask that upon detecting REM pulsed red light into the dreamer's eyes. Both devices have had some good results.[10]

More recent studies, in particular those of Ursula Voss and colleagues at Goethe University, Frankfurt, have shown lucidity to be a hybrid state of consciousness with features of REM sleep and wakefulness blended together.[11] This correlates with an increase of gamma activity (particularly in the 40 Hz frequency band) in the frontal lobe, as well as a global increase of awake-like brainwave coherence. Lucid dreaming represents a special "switching on" of what American biologist Gerald Edelman called secondary consciousness,[12] which he considered to be dependent on language. Using this research as a foundation, subsequent sleep lab experiments have shown that spontaneous bursts of lucidity during ordinary REM sleep (and even in self-reported nonlucid dreamers) can be provoked by sending low-intensity electrical stimulation (using the 40 Hz frequency in particular) through the frontal and temporal lobe (transcranial alternating current stimulation, or tACS).[13] I think this is one of the most promising experimental areas of research for a future of therapeutic lucid dream induction.

I first spoke to Daniel Oldis about his research into dream speech several years ago; in fact, I reached out to him after I had a dream about a film I had made (in a dream) called *A New Theory of Deep Sleep*. Daniel is an early contemporary researcher on the subject of lucid dreams and conducts sleep lab experiments, researching circadian rhythms, dream time perception and dream consciousness; in particular he studies and experiments with various ways of recording and communicating with dreamers when they are within a dream. Following Daniel's inspired correspondence, I experimented with speaking in my own dreams. I tried to feel more consciously into my own voice box in dreams. Dream recording has been a fascination of mine since childhood, since my first ideas about recording my own dreams and making them into a film so that I could make my friends watch them. The visual reconstruction of a dream realm still seems to me to be the ultimate magic.

In a lucid dream experience, the richness and clarity of any given dream scene can feel overwhelming. This is often why people end up jolting themselves out of sleep, and why so many lucid dreamers begin their journey as children, having very real-feeling nightmares. The intensity of this realness is exciting and enlivening, and it seems to signal powerfully to the self-aware aspect of ourselves.

LUCID DREAM TECHNIQUES AND SLEEP HYGIENE

Sleep hygiene is a vital dream technology that cannot be underestimated. I have sleep and dream rituals that I practice every night that help me relax. I think it is deeply important to approach sleeping and dreaming with reverence. We should mentally elevate it as a therapeutic health treatment, a deeply creative, expressive art form, an expression of a working relationship with the universe and a spiritual and prophetic practice.

There are a variety of techniques that I use to stabilize lucidity within a dream. Sometimes I hold my dream eyelids open and drink in the dream scene. Sometimes I spin my dream body, concentrating all of my powers of mind into the dream reality. Sometimes the opposite action is more beneficial. It helps to hold on loosely to the dream, with a sort of soft focus, until the waking mind has returned to a dreaming equilibrium.

Optimal Sleep Hygiene Practices

- Try to sleep for a minimum of eight hours a night. When it comes to dream memory and recall, at least eight hours is necessary for most people, although everyone has a unique circadian rhythm fingerprint.
- When you fall asleep, the first sleep cycles are the shortest. Your body's priority here is non-REM sleep for cellular regeneration and detoxification. As your sleep progresses, your sleep cycles become

longer, with maximum opportunities for lucid dreaming in the longest REM cycles just before awakening in the morning.

- It's easier to get eight hours a night if you minimize caffeine and establish a regular bedtime that is no later than 11:00 p.m.

- Turn off devices and screens by 7:00 or 8:00 p.m. Use blue light filters to minimize sensitivity and overstimulation during the day.

- Do not eat a heavy meal before going to sleep. Fasting is excellent for dreaming.

- Avoid alcohol. As a depressant, its lingering, dampening effects can take months to wear off completely.

- Keep your bedroom dark and silent. Create a sleep temple in your own home and make your bedroom a sacred space. Try to restrict your bedroom activities to sleeping and intimacy only.

- Bathe before sleeping. Dr. Google reveals several legit references that a hot bath does indeed lower body core temperature, which is good for sound and restful sleep. Often our sleep is disturbed by spikes in temperature, and this can feed into distressing dream content and disturb us further. Epsom salts in the bath can be very helpful for promoting restful sleep.

- Bedding and a mattress made of natural materials are best. Synthetic fibers and memory foam mattresses can make us feel hot and uncomfortable. Their lack of breathability is unhealthy for the skin and nervous system. When we're hot, we will often have distressing or anxious dreams, as our inner dream vision attempts to create a narrative from the sensory landscape of our body.

- Cannabis and antidepressants can suppress REM sleep. Be mindful of this and have afternoon naps, meditate, or try sleep hypnosis sessions if possible to encourage dreaming.

- Do not watch horror movies! It sounds obvious, but if you watch, read, or think about scary, gory, or horrifying events, you will very likely incorporate these visual elements into your dreams and have nightmares. In general, think about what media and visual input you consume. Think about it the same way you would think about the food you should eat if you want to be healthy.

- If you have a nightmare or come across a scary presence in the sleep state, remember that your dream characters are powered by your feelings and thoughts. Do not fight a dream character. This will just exhaust you and give them more power. Neutralize the negative feelings in your dream body and try to project a feeling of love onto this shadow. You might experience an amazing alchemical transformation, and the scary character might morph into a perfectly loving being. It may evaporate, transmute into something more positive, or it might be absorbed by your dreaming avatar.

- In dreams, try eating and drinking. Often a dream food or drink can act as an agent of transformation, as depicted in Alice in Wonderland. It's even possible to experience dream inebriation, a dream catalyst that can be helpful sometimes. I have often wondered if this experience might have been the inspiration for ideas about not partaking of refreshments in the underworld, as we see in the myths of Persephone and others.

- Any activity or supplement that improves your memory will likely improve your chances of attaining dream lucidity, as becoming lucid in a dream is really remembering who and where you are.

- If you wake up and haven't had a lucid dream, just try going back to sleep until you do.

- Play word and memory games. I have found Scrabble to be especially good. The configuration of words from random letters works similarly to the dreaming mind's way of language-processing and word identification.

- Read novels and write stories, especially magical realism. Research has shown that when we read novels and immerse ourselves in reading fiction, our neural pathways are altered as a result of us imagining ourselves somewhere else.

- Think about your past dreams, read old dream journal entries, or map out the world of your dreams. Draw a map of your desired imaginal realm or embellish an existing one. Imagine and fantasize. Imagining is a dream workout!

- Cultivate a crush on someone. Having a crush or a deeply romantic attraction is great for dreaming. Our wish-fulfilling dream minds want to bring us the object of our affection.

- Go on holiday or get a holiday mind-set. When we are on holiday, time seems to pass more slowly. We often experience a slightly altered state of consciousness as we drink in new and novel surroundings. I call this exotic consciousness. Try to encourage this exotic way of seeing things in your everyday life.

- Write down your dreams as soon as you have them. Take note of the words—there is often a lot of punning and wordplay in dreams. Analyze them, think about what message they are trying to communicate. Recording dreams is a dynamic process that strengthens future dream experiences and memories. The act of writing down a dream remembers it to conscious memory and strengthens the architectural structures of our inner memory palace.

- Try sleep hypnosis for an afternoon nap or when falling asleep at night. Sleep hypnosis constitutes a sort of curated sleep experience, where you can surrender to the voice of the guide and allow them to take you on a guided sleep journey. It can be especially useful if you are suffering from anxiety or insomnia to practice during the day as there is less pressure and worry about falling asleep. Always make a point to record your imaginal impressions and experiences however transient or vague.

- Use scent to tap in to the interconnectedness of the olfactory and memory brain regions.[14] I have experimented using certain scents to evoke particular memories in dreams. For example, the smell of freshly cut grass might remind you of being a child during summer holidays, so if you take a nap in a freshly mown meadow you might find yourself dreaming of your childhood. Certain essential oils are known to have a calming effect on the nervous system—vervain, frankincense, and cardamom I find to be especially soothing, but a lot of this is down to personal taste.

DREAM CREATIVITY

Using your dreams as the fecund creative source they naturally are is a rewarding practice that can help deepen your awareness of your psyche.

If you use your dream symbols as totems, motifs, and themes in your own art and creatives practices, this will strengthen their appearance in the dream realm. Explore and analyze these symbols; research their history, meaning, and application. Your dreaming mind will develop and expand your art and your thinking. Creating this feedback system between the dreaming and waking worlds can help you cultivate a conscious dream eloquence and enriches your experience of the world. Our dreams are the oeuvre of our soul.

DIVINE DREAMS

We humans used to worship the sun. Whether we see the solar disk as female or male, the sun is our life-giving ruler. As the primary source of light for our planet, it governs us and is a living, conscious entity. The moon was traditionally regarded as the guardian of the night, and its reflective light quality was seen in the luminous realm of dreams. What rules us now?

I think it's very important for humanity to reestablish a sense of the divine nature of reality, a sense of the living spirit of nature. These are excellent themes to explore in dreams.

Some of the positive things that happened as a result of the social isolation strategies and lockdowns of COVID-19 were that more and more people began spending time alone in nature; people also had more time to dream. During this unknown and unpredictable event, people were bonding deeply with their local areas of nature and truly appreciating the opportunity for health and the freedom these natural places offer. These places remained safe, trusted refuges. In effect, we returned to our sacred groves.

In solitude, communion with nature can be especially influential on the human spirit. When we are alone, we are silent enough to hear nature's voice. When are still enough we can see her subtle emanations. When I contemplate the most profound and awe-inspiring moments of my life, they are always when I have been alone in nature. Nature is the Divine. Birdsong is the Divine. The sunrise is Heaven. Unfolding plants still know how to worship, to live and die for the sun. We are living in a Garden of Eden, and whatever we take from nature, nature will one day take back from us.

The earliest religions were animistic, nature-worshipping cultures, and I do think we may be ready to return to something similar. I believe environmental movements sometimes flounder because they are rooted in politics and scientism. Nature is spiritual.

On the positive side, the darkness and quiet of lockdowns gave us a deeper understanding of the mind-set of ancient people when it comes to the joy of spring. The quiet was extraordinary—it opened up a whole new dimension of connection. The birds sing to us. Spring's divine golden light and effervescent warmth bless us. The explosive rupturing of the soil that reveals the hidden color of life all around us and the synchronistic rising of sap within us brings new feelings of energy, vitality, lust, and joy. The verdant landscape of spring is an unrivaled expression of the glory of the sentient, orgasmic earth, the world delighting in itself.

There is also the matter of just how oblivious we are to the extent of our diminished natural resources, known as the shifting baseline syndrome.[15] Our ancestors and even fairly recent previous generations in most cases experienced an enormously richer biodiversity in the world around them, one with significantly larger populations of species across all taxonomic classes. Just imagine how potent this experience of spring was for them without any indoor distractions and without artificial light, pointless office jobs, central heating and air conditioning, and supermarkets, without Netflix or Tinder. Spring was and is just pure, unabated earthly ecstasy. What are the best moments of life if not those moments when we are in harmony with the whole of nature? Only in nature can we truly live. Nature provides the only cure.

DREAM SEX AND LOVE

Poetry leads to the same place as all forms of eroticism—to the blending and fusion of separate objects. It leads us to eternity, it leads us to death, and through death to continuity. Poetry is eternity; the sun matched with the sea.

— Georges Bataille, *Erotism: Death and Sensuality*

At the florescence of orgasm it is common to experience a brief loss of self-awareness. Romantically referred to as *la petite mort,* literally "the little death," this trance state can be an ideal way to access a lucid dream. Ecstatic trance states have been tapped for millennia by priestesses, prophetesses, and seers to inspire oracular insight. Ecstatic states can also be accessed through sexual arousal,[16] adoration, dance, music, psychedelics, and many other consciousness-altering techniques and substances.

Orgasm alters consciousness, acts as a powerful analgesic, and has been associated with the activation of certain key brain regions responsible for modulating perception of reality and time.[17] In the deep sense of timeless peace that unfolds throughout your body post-orgasm, you are in a unique position to practice the art of lucid dreaming without falling into a deep sleep. In the dream realm, supersubtle, subconscious, multisensory perceptions of your inner landscapes and immediate environment converge to create elaborate visual dreamscapes.

Encouraging desire is one way to increase the chances of a lucid episode. One common impetus of lucid dreaming is love. When we feel strong desire or elevated romantic adoration, we feel especially activated. The object of our desire provokes special expansions of our consciousness. Like arcing plasma filaments and the radiant curlicues of the sun, the tendrils of our awareness reach beyond ourselves to merge with our beloved.

As poetry arouses the mystic's soul, love arouses extrasensory perceptions and vivid impressions of beauty. These heightened emotional experiences are easily transferred and realized in the dream realm.

DREAMS AND ETERNITY

My childhood dreams provoked within me a deep curiosity, a deep wondering about how lucid dreaming could provide a direct experience of an immortal spirit. It gave me the idea that something of me might perpetuate after my physical death. That in developing and strengthening lucid awareness, I might transcend my mortal existence.

The dream realm is a place to tap in to universal remembrance, to access a mythological field of ancestral memory. The dream exists in a realm where no time is felt to exist, where the art of seeing is woven into the fabric of the landscape. It offers the experience of being an all-creative spirit. We perceive in the dream world with every atom of our being. We can witness the past, present, and future simultaneously. We can observe close-up and far away. We can take up multiple vantage points. We can fly.

When we fall asleep, we visit the place we emerged from at birth, the place we shall return to when we die. Advanced dreaming skills might help us navigate in this other world, but it is not enough to simply dream. To dream meaningfully requires divine inspiration. Dreams offer us a space for communion with the divine. They deliver us to a nonphysical realm in which we can consummate our relationship with the Godhead. To dream well, then, is to say before we sleep, "World, stars, I adore you!"

Initiatic Story: My House Is Arkady

In the Sacred Grove, the Old Woman directs me to the birch tree she wants to lie under. After resting on the soft moss awhile she says to me that she is ready to die. She says she can feel the birch tree drawing her up with the earth. The birds are silent for us, so we listen and we can hear the birch's sap rushing through its trunk. She knows its language better than I do, so she smiles.

This Sacred Grove is untouchable. We cannot take any herb, water, or wagtail from it. This place is preserved for the nature spirits so that they may reach their full potency. This is the place where we come to appreciate them, to absorb their unadulterated energies. We only enter the Sacred Grove to nurture them with our offerings and give them the best outpourings of our hearts. The Mari children come here to sleep among nature's feelers. In their sleep, they learn her ways of speaking.

The Sacred Grove energizes us and nourishes our souls. In this zone, we walk barefoot on the forest floor so that the earth can really know our footprints.

In the forest along the way, before we had arrived at the Sacred Grove, I had tapped a birch for water. This water I now trickled into the Old Woman's mouth from my flask. Her head is so heavy in my hand. I can feel her soul already sending its tendrils into the ground like roots.

The light of the sacred grove is utterly divine, as though it has passed through an emerald. The full canopy of overlapping, sticky, lime-green birch leaves shelters us from a hazing rain. A chilled morning mist rises over the ferns, over the mosses and bright blue squills of the forest floor. The standing trunks of the birch trees are luminous fingers. They emanate a terrestrial tenderness. The birch are a family of ancient beings, and they have established a breathing cathedral of pure benevolence on the Earth. They stand always ready to hold a ritual. Their arrangement is the fulfillment of a natural seraphic order, an order that emanates from the Great Light.

Whenever I am away from the Sacred Grove, I do my best to conjure up the peaceful feeling that I find there. I recall the roots and the deep, earthy perfume of lichen, the fragrance of fruiting mushroom bodies, wild strawberries, squashed bilberries; the smoky, aromatic, and metallic tang of birch pitch drifting in from the village. I love the sweet and peaty smell of chaga and bird nests in the treetops, the wet grass and musky odor of black bear rubbed on a tree trunk, the warm mist of pine needle tea stirred with honey in old wooden cups. My senses swim in the midst of all this natural glory. Even as I lie in my bed at night, I am overcome at times when I surrender to the vivid recollection of the Sacred Grove's riches. I loved all of this even before I moved full-time to live with nature. I came to the Mari when I was forty-four.

For so many around the world, the people of nature, like the Mari, had become true beacons of real light. The veil had fallen from our beady, city-screened eyes. The old gods of these people became our new gods. And the gods were vivified and enlivened by the new attention we gave them. We knew we needed gods again. We knew we needed the forces of nature. We knew we needed the lick of immortal adoration on our hearts. We knew we needed a soul. We needed an afterlife, too.

The people of nature, those who dwelled inside of her, they have stayed true to their gods all along. People gradually turned away from burned-out lives. They gave up the work and distractions that bathed them daily in an unholy light. They left the streets and shops that had jangled their nerves with sharp and jagged sounds.

Many of us returned to the Great Light, to the Goddess, and to the Sacred Grove. We were welcomed back. The Mari taught me and my daughter how to dissolve into the forest, and we now live in the New House of Arkady. We live on the edge of the Sacred Grove and close to the mountain and the river of the Goddess . . .

The Old Woman is in her funeral dress. She has shining silver coins sewn over her chest. These will pay her way in the afterlife. She will pay with jingling and mirrors, with the *idea* of money. The afterlife is a realm of ideas, I think. She tells me she will come and find me in my dreams. She says she will tell me all about what it's like for her. She asks me to bring her food sometimes. She asks me to pour vodka on her grave when I remember her.

Then she passes painlessly into the earth. I feel her trickle through my fingers. On her final breath, a small butterfly is carried over to me, a blue. There is the gray whisper of rainbow iridescence on its precious powdery wings. The clouds above the world tear themselves apart to reveal the full force of the Great Light, and a viridian brightness floods the Sacred Grove. That whisper of iridescence on the butterfly's wing, it shines and rainbows the air.

I know now the Old Woman has had a good death. The Old Woman was a good sorcerer after all.

o o o

Meditations

The following transcriptions are the companions to the seven audio meditations, which are available for download at

audio.innertraditions.com/InDrMy

The individual recordings each require about forty-five minutes of listening time, and as mentioned earlier, I suggest creating a sacred space within your home or out in nature that is dedicated to your private dream incubation rituals. It is worth creating a serene and relaxing environment in which distractions and outside noise can easily be minimized and basic sleep hygiene protocol followed.

PHASE ONE: CHRYSALIS

You are standing in a smooth tunnel of sandstone. A gorge scoured out over millennia by running rivers has smoothed and rounded the stone as water has coursed and swirled through, creating this maze.

The stone is dry now. Run your fingertips across the crystalline surface, feeling tiny points of quartz warming as they sparkle and reflect the sounds of footsteps echoing along this channel, sounding hollow and dry. In the distance you can hear water trickling . . . babbling into puddles and over stones . . . the rocks rushing with bubbling water, receiving heads and leaves . . . the tips of the leaves of the trees and plants, dipping their heads in . . . as though they're being baptized by this divine, flowing water. And there is a flash! A kingfisher bird darts along the bank, glistening, radiant blue and orange, flashing jewel-like. Your eyes follow this bird now . . . following this bird as it moves swiftly along the banks of the river, moving with the flowing water . . . rushes, rushes with the currents and eddies . . . and disappears into his nest hole in the bank. You imagine yourself standing on the threshold of this tiny nest hole in the rock. It allows you to enter the home of the kingfisher. And you imagine yourself now very small, small as this small bird, and you're stepping into the darkness of this vast cave hidden on the riverbank. The walls are made of banked-up mud, lightened by the sun.

You see handprints and carvings, curving lines of animals and birds. Surrounded by these drawings, the paintings come to life before your eyes. You can feel the energy of their creators swirling around you . . . You feel the earth beneath your feet . . . You see large leaves and forms and plants along the riverbank, and hanging on one broken stem is the glistening thread that supports a heavy paper chrysalis. Inside this chrysalis you see the beginnings of new life. A new precious and beautiful life is contained within this capsule . . . a capsule that contains the very elixir of transformation that you require. And you walk over to this chrysalis, this cocoon, which swings in the breeze, reverberating with the rumbling stream beneath you. You bring your fingers toward this capsule, this chrysalis . . . Cool is its papery texture, its lines and sections. Grip the chrysalis. When you pull it away from the twig snapping the silken thread that connects it. Place this chrysalis in your mouth. You feel its papery shell crush between your teeth. You taste the bitter essence of transformation, the liquid alchemy. A fluid of magic is on your tongue and now runs down your throat into your body . . . energizing, transforming . . . inner alchemy at work. This is the sacrament of the dream realm. You feel your body absorbing and accepting, surrendering to this medicine.

Allow its power to flow into your cells, to your organs. It soothes your vascular system, calms your nervous system. It floods the channels of your brain. You feel a great sense of peace, the deep workings of magic and healing. You feel very calm, very serene. And you are touched by this deep, divine medicine. This panacea loves your body . . . your body is recalibrating, purifying, cleansing. Your spirit body is lifted up on the back of the kingfisher in this bed, luminous with the deep green-blue of this bird's feathers . . . radiant, celestial feathers, iridescent in the sunlight, as you are lifted up into the sky . . . light and easy, as though you yourself were a feather gliding on the breeze . . .

PHASE TWO: THE HEAD

The head is lying on rich, red earth, emptied of spirit . . . flesh soft, dragging off the bones, the essence, the essence of your life, the energy of your soul departed now . . . an echo of your previous habitation . . . In this body of flesh and bone, this echo seeps into the earth beneath it as your soul flies high above the clouds with the birds and the insects, the butterflies and dragonflies and flies and beetles . . .

You feel free and light, aware of that which you have left behind as your remains slowly disintegrate, slowly merge with the earth, enriching the earth. From your vantage point high in the sky, high above the cool breezes, the chill of the clouds, breath of flapping bird wings, you see your body and you watch it slowly decompose. Slowly and gradually comes the covering greenness . . . Rot becomes food for worms, for insects, for birds . . . for small animals, for bigger animals . . . And the birds' beaks tear at the flesh, and the wolf's fangs sink into the muscle. The worms and maggots writhe in the flesh. The mice nibble on your bare bones. The sun beats down on your corpse, melting away all of the remaining flesh and tissue until you are a gleaming white skeleton, polished bone, washed by light and water, gleaming and reflecting. Look into the sockets of what once was your eyes, the black pits that remain. It is the element of air that finally carries you away, finally lifts you up and distributes you through the ethers, over the soil, onto the leaves of trees, even into the nostrils of your descendants. You enrich the world, you merge and become one with the matter of the planet, your spirit travels across the land. A weightless body, you feel a connection to all things divine and celestial. You move fluidly through the air . . . able to observe all things of the heavens, able to pick up the thoughts and feelings of the sum total of all conscious awareness on the planet.

Somehow you tap in to the cosmic web of memory, the web of eternal remembrance . . . You are an ancestor and you are a future descendant. You travel all over the world. You feel the oceans, the soil, the insects, the birds, the animals. You feel your life coursing through the veins of a tree as it draws nourishment up through the ground. You feel the delight the tree experiences as its leaves absorb the radiance of the sun. You feel the rhythm of the oceans and rivers, the inhalation and exhalation, the tides and the currents. You become one with the great rhythm of the planet.

You immerse yourself in this feeling of bliss, this feeling of ecstasy, of belonging, of coming home and remembering . . . And as you feel a belonging with this planet, a silver thread from your heart connects you and reminds you of your place in the universe, of your place in all time and space . . .

Of the imaginal reality, the cosmos in your new, eternal, feeling mind, you remember all sayings, you remember all futures. You feel and sense all time and space simultaneously. You are an immortal, eternal being in a timeless dimension. You recollect the visions of your gleaming, bleached skull, and you recognize that your tiny life on Earth was but a fraction of your total experience of reality.

PHASE THREE: THRESHOLD

You are floating in complete and utter darkness. Your body feels weightless, very relaxed and calm . . . Buoyed by this obsidian abyss, the air, the space around you, has a texture, and you can feel the body of this nothingness around you, holding you . . .

Now you see in the distance two tall gateposts. These gateposts are made out of tall bundles of reeds with a loop at the top. They emanate an ethereal and moonlike light and glow faintly green. In the pitch-black of this abyss, filled almost as though you are seeing from the other side of your eyes . . . There is a reflection of reality, rather than reality itself. You approach these gateposts silently, and once you get closer you see tiny threads of green light being sucked into the fabric of the gate, into the center of the space in between. The gateposts are a portal into another dimension. You slowly cross this threshold, and you feel yourself being magnetically pulled into this other realm, this other space. Time evaporates. Your body runs like a vapor into the underworld.

In this dark realm, you are beyond time, beyond space, beneath material reality. You're in the realm of all life, the source of all creation, of all gestation and development, of evolution. All things must die, all things must be reborn. The cycle of life and death sinks to its lowest point in the underworld, its deepest, most creative and nourishing depths. You are here now in this realm. Here are all the creatures of destruction and decay, all those that take life between their jaws, that recycle energy, that live for blood and rot and decay. And you are here. You are here to witness the goddess of creation, the goddess of regeneration. She has the power of creativity and life. This is the realm we shall all enter upon death. And this is the realm from which we emerge at birth.

As you look around you, you can see many large insects. Wading birds with long legs and probing beaks stalk the air above you. You are tiny in this realm, as though a microbe making your way through a labyrinth of decay and rot. Breaking down to be rebuilt . . . The earth writhes with life and activity. Worms, beetles, maggots, and their larva emerge, chewing, consuming, absorbing all, to bring new life into being, all of these creatures working together to homogenize energy, to unify creation. You make your way through this maze, through this labyrinth. The darkness is warm, nurturing, the air thick around your face and eyes. And you see her now.

Towering, a giant, luminous body, is the goddess Inanna. Naked, powerful, magnificent, and terrifying. She is drawing up all of the energy of the underworld through the claws of her owl feet to the tips of the talons on her fingers. The roots of her hair vibrate with all the energy and power that she absorbs. She stands on the back of a black beast, a feline creature whose spine is bowed under the weight of supporting the Great Goddess. His fangs are glistening in the strange light of the underworld. Inanna leans forward, draws her ax from her back, and cleaves you in two. Your body peels apart, splitting down the center, folding over onto the earth, which is awaiting you with a million greedy mouths that take you in, begin to chew you and break you down. And Inanna whispers into your right ear. Everything that dies in the underworld will live again. The creatures of the earth turn you over in their soil and bodies. They mix you up with the elements, confuse your cells and atoms, and prepare to reconfigure you for another life.

PHASE FOUR: EYE

Feel the swirling vortex between your eyebrows. Imagine a new eye in your forehead just there. Imagine that you are looking into your inner world through this eye, sucking in all of its details through your third pupil. Delight in the forward motion into and through your own inner universe. The Divine has eyes, and your third eye is a cell in the body of the Divine. And through this eye, this sacred and divine reorganization, you can unravel the fabric of reality.

Absorb the divine secrets of creation. Make your offerings to the immortal gods. Witness the play of life on Earth and in the heavens . . .

At your altar to the Goddess, you make offerings of beautiful flower blossoms, heavy with closed and open heads. The blue water lilies are vibrant with violet-blue hues and bright gold; they are a symbol of the sun, a reflection of the divine force of life on Earth. We place these heavy heads as fixed gems on your altar. You burn the sacred resin of frankincense and myrrh. Feel the smoke curl around your hair. Send its feelers to your nose and ears and mouth. You can taste the residue of sacred smoke on your tongue. You are purified by the smoke. You are bathed in holy water, you are cleansed. You are pure and ready to receive a vision from the gods. Eyes resonate with the perfected inner sanctum of this temple. You see the body of the Goddess, a stone statue come to life. Her soft, gentle face is benevolent, graceful, elegant, loving. The perfection of her visage fills your heart with joy.

Your heart now feels warm and full of love, as though it were a pot overflowing with warm spirits and energy, brimming and bubbling over with delight, with ecstasy and happiness. This good, perfect feeling rises up through your body, through the base of your spine, feeding into your heart a glowing light. These points of light within your body connect you with all things in the cosmos. A natural, divine light . . . This light moves through your body, rising up like a wonderful wave of healing, ecstasy, bliss, joy, wonder, and awe . . .

You experience exquisite sensations rolling up your spine along the vertebrae, spreading out across your rib cage and rippling through your muscles, through your skin, through all of your organs. An exquisite liquid divinity melds together the material elements of your body into one rapturous glory. You are full of life. As this elixir expands and flows into every corner and crevice of your body, you feel all trauma and tension and stress melt away, so the energy can now flow smoothly and cleanly through your body. You are a pure conduit to the heavens, and your energy flows freely now, from the very tips of your toes, passing through all the energy centers of your body smoothly, easily, healthily, contentedly, joyfully, ecstatically. You are flowing like a smooth, unencumbered spring river, running with pure, healthy energy, all the way through your body up to the crown of your head.

You feel so blissful . . . You feel a sensation of warm sparkling all across the top of your head, spreading out across your scalp . . . This is tantalizing and delicious, sparkling and effervescent, this tingling sensation all across your scalp, from the top of your head to the edges of your hairline, around your ears, and down the back of your neck. A sparkling, tingling, healing power moves with your will, merges with your own power . . .

PHASE FIVE: BEE

You are in the bottom of a beautiful gorge. A river murmurs contentedly to your left, passing through the dappled shade of cypress trees. You walk along a twisting path through the trees, stroking their rough grooved trunks as you pass underneath them, listening to the birds and the animals. All are finding their way through the undergrowth or flying out, flying out of the treetops, bouncing along the branches, rustling their leaves.

The sky is pure blue and as bright as the sun is radiant. The sun beats down on the outside of the shade, drying and cracking the red earth. Shining mountains roll up toward the sky from this gorge, a channel of nourishment from the Goddess. Her power as a mountain is strong, fixed, electric, and energizing and you breathe deeply now . . .

A fresh, fragrant, herb-scented air fills the gorge. This is nourishment from the Goddess. You step down toward the river that is rushing at your feet and you fill your cup with this pure and glorious water. Dip your cup into this rushing water from the Goddess, from the heart of her mountain, from the heart of her. You fill your cup and lift the cool water to your lips. You drink deeply now, and as you drink deeply, you feel your body responding to this healing water of memory as it flows down your throat, refreshing your body, bringing your body back into alignment with the Earth, the water, and the fire of life, you feel grateful and happy and content to have this connection. To be able to drink of the air, to be able to drink of the Goddess, to be able to imbibe the essence, the divine sacred female power that creates life. The Goddess gave birth to you. Your head leans back to take the water. Deeply you feel its coolness running down your throat . . .

You notice the temple standing on top of the next hill and you see a honey buzzard flying in the blue, between the red-painted columns. Following this buzzard with your eyes, you decide to visit this temple. You drank from the Goddess, and now you must go and make your peace in her sacred precinct. You must offer your mind and body to the Goddess, you must lie on the stones of her temple and feel her power . . . and receive her message in your sleep.

So you walk toward this temple, as though you are in trance, being drawn ahead by the Goddess herself. An irresistible power leads you up the hillside along the path, passing through the towering red pillars of the temple. You feel their breathing as you pass into the shade of the temple, through the portico, and out into a wide arena paved with giant stones, warm and worn by many visitors. You feel the warmth of the stones against your bare back. You close your eyes, allowing the gentle breezes and the aromatics of this beautiful temple in the forest to gently percolate through all of your senses. You are guided to a great tree. And in this great tree there is the beautiful Goddess, her face carved in stone.

She opens her mouth, receives the sweet honey that you pour on her tongue, and from her mouth, from deep within her being, comes the sound of bees buzzing, vibrant with life. They are rich with knowing. They swarm around her face, and they crawl across your hands to your lips, and you can taste the pollen on their legs and the sweetness of their honey. They whisper in their buzzing, their buzzing murmurs, a message to you . . . whispering in your ears, speaking and buzzing of your future. They reveal the secrets of the underworld, future visions they've had in the Valley of the Goddess. Their knowing is a collective. They know the connectedness of all things, the connectedness of mind and of consciousness, of love and energy. And they love you, just as the Goddess loves you . . .

PHASE SIX: SNAKE

You find yourself standing on top of a dark set of steps that lead you underground, into a dark chamber. It is a sacred precinct. The god Asklepios, a healing and benevolent god, along with his attendant serpents, live in this dark chamber. In this place you may contact him, you may touch the god and experience his influence. His influence can spread throughout your body, providing healing, comfort, and perfection.

This stairwell leads through a circular temple—the tholos. The thymele sitting at the centre of the sanctuary is surrounded by walls and within a circular path. You are one of many bodies on these paths, and you spiral into it. You are aware of your feet leading you down some stone steps, carefully carrying you into the god's sacred inner sanctum. A most important ritual space, this entire sanctuary is the divine home of the god. You can hear the music of lyres and the gentle, melodius singing of hymns to the gods. Smoke winds its way up this path and over the steps, blanketing each step with a pure white, holy smoke. And every step you take, one after the other, you become more deeply relaxed. You feel yourself synchronizing to the steps, feeling into the dark, your body easing down this corridor, disappearing from the world of light, flowing into the world of darkness and regeneration.

In this realm, the god and his serpent wrap themselves around you. You are harmonized, your body fixed, your mind purified to remove corruptions. You step slowly now into this dark chamber and you see the gorgeous Asklepios, a giant sitting on his throne, his dog at his side. Asklepios rests his hand on top of the dog's head. A snake's powerful body curls around a branch. You are held firmly, planted in the grass. This is a statue, a living, breathing statue made from plates of ivory and wood, oiled and living, threaded together with gold, encrusted in jewels. The god is crowned, adorned, and adored. You fall to your knees at the feet of Asklepios. You look down at his toes—his feet are perfectly carved, immaculate, pure. You see his flesh move with the breath of life. You see the snake inch its way up the branch. Then from beyond there is the sound of steps, and a gorgeous living, breathing, brilliant goddess walks toward you, shining like gold. She extends her fingertips toward you and takes your hand, leading you toward her, bringing you down even farther, to another realm beyond this chamber, into the very heart of consciousness, to the gates of creation. You must pass in dreams and death to emerge truly alive, truly conscious. She draws you toward her, her gold glittering. She emanates wisdom, memory, and knowing. She who is pure gold and gleaming like the sun. She reminds you now to remember, always remember, what has happened before, and remember also how the world will unfold in the future.

The goddess leads you into a dark realm, the dark realm of radiance, where there are no stars and there is no sun. Light glows from all things. The shining white trunk of a cypress tree glows brilliantly. Before you water gushes out from the tree's roots, the water of Lethe, of forgetting. The feel of moss. And I guide you along this path, past the shining trunk of the white cypress tree to a great pool of moonlit water that glows, in the darkness. This is the water of life . . . Drink now to remember . . .

PHASE SEVEN: SACRED GROVE

You are standing in the Sacred Grove, a tranquil and beautiful forest. The trees and the plants here are all divine manifestations of the power behind the universe, the creative force behind reality. Their forms and shapes are an expression of the Divine. In this place you can tap directly into that power. In this untouched, pristine, beautiful forest, the Divine can flow directly into your body. In this place the elements merge with the things of the world, and you, too, merge as you lie against the roots of the trees.

Underneath the canopy of leaves of overlapping greenness, beautiful emerald light streams through the forest. The sky is augmented by the trees. The Sacred Grove is our alchemical liminal zone, a place between the Divine and the mortal. In this place you are protected. This place is a sanctuary, a peaceful zone of no harm. You are held by the Earth in this place, surrounded and corrected by her elements, touched and nourished by the living fibers of the world. You lean back against the shining trunk of a silver birch tree, and you feel the vibrations of sap rising through its trunk. You hear the gush and the rush of this vital fluid. It passes in front of your ears, and you feel how this tree lives and breathes, how it moves slowly and easily through time and space. This tree has a great conscious, moving life. Beneath this beautiful tree, mycelial networks spread out, embracing the land, extracting and delivering nourishment and sending chemical signals. They are breaking down all that decomposes as part of the cycle of life. And life emerges once again, new, vibrant, reborn. Lie back on this rich, ancient earth, land that exists on the bones of our ancestors. You feel all of history and all of memory contained within this soil. You dig your fingers into this soil and feel this history and all of these memories between your fingers. You are aware now of your place in this beautiful, intricate system, your place in the network. The divine light shines the way, the light we return to when we die and the light we emerge from when we're born. Take a deep breath now and breathe in the living essence of the Sacred Grove, these beloved trees . . .

This humble earth represents the most sacred and precious resource on the planet. This clean, pure water that trickles and runs from the spring is holy and contains the memories of every living being on Earth. You know now that you must always return to the Sacred Grove. It represents all that is precious and all that is important in the world . . . the harmony and health of nature. At the roots of this precious tree you feel everything around you, living and breathing in harmony, in health and vitality. Surrounded by harmony and vitality, this tree has the power to recalibrate you, to bring you back to your true nature, to bring you back into harmony.

All you need do is forget everything, forget everything now and surrender yourself to the power, magic, and alchemy of the beautiful Sacred Grove . . . Return in your mind now to the beautiful, Sacred Grove . . . Submit all of your senses to appreciating and understanding, knowing and loving the Sacred Grove . . .

You feel the beat of a butterfly's wings on your face, and you recognize the voice and power of all living things, the inner alchemy that dwells within all conscious entities. There is still great potential for change and transformation. As you submit to the power of the Sacred Grove, you feel this inner alchemy working on you as an elixir of transformation in the form of a capsule. The capsule cracks open within you and floods your senses with wonder . . .

Notes

INTRODUCTION. KA, THE CREATIVE SPIRIT

1. Johnsen and Lohmann, "The Physics and Neurobiology of Magnetoreception," 703–12.
2. Gehring and Rosbash, "The Coevolution of Blue-Light Photoreception."
3. Dresler et al., "Neural Correlates of Dream Lucidity," 1017–20.
4. Baird, Castelnovo, and Gosseries, "Frequent Lucid Dreaming."
5. Timmermann et al., "Psychedelics Alter Metaphysical Beliefs."
6. Scarpelli et al., "Functional Role."
7. Kraehenmann, "Neurophenomenological Comparison," 1032–42.
8. Vicente et al., "Enhanced Interplay."
9. Noegel and Szpakowska, "'Word Play,'" 193–212.
10. Patel, Reddy, and Araujo, *Physiology, Sleep Stages*.
11. Hao, Kaisheng, and Lingnan, "Where You Are."
12. Loddo et al., "Disorders of arousal."
13. Sandu and Nistor, "Digital Dementia."
14. Dawes et al., "Cognitive Profile."
15. Berns et al., "Short- and long-Term Effects," 590–600.
16. Clinton, "Epiphany," 85–109.

PHASE ONE. THE DAWN OF DREAMS

1. Aubert et al., "Palaeolithic Cave Art," 254–57.
2. Dalton, "Lion Man Takes Pride of Place."
3. Henshilwood et al., "A 100,000-Year-Old Ochre-Processing Workshop," 219–22.
4. Kenny et al., "A Late Paleocene Age."

5. Murchie et al., "Collapse of the Mammoth-Steppe."

6. Zadra, Desjardins, and Marcotte, "Evolutionary Function of Dreams."

7. Berlucchi and Buchtel, "Neuronal Plasticity," 309–17.

8. Rochberg, "Personifications and Metaphors," 475–85.

9. Bégouen, "The Magic Origin," 5–19.

10. Noegel, "Dreams and Dream Interpreters."

11. Elce, Handjaras, and Bernardi, "The Language of Dreams," 495–514.

12. Price-Williams and Gaines, "The Dreamtime and Dreams," 373–88.

13. Grosman, Munro, and Belfer-Cohen, "A 12,000-Year-Old Shaman Burial," 17665–669.

PHASE TWO. INTO THE BRONZE AGE

1. Knitter et al., "Göbekli Tepe: A Brief Description."

2. Bar-Yosef and Valla, "The Natufian Culture," 433–36.

3. Darvill, "Keeping Time at Stonehenge," 1–17.

4. Sweatman and Tsikritsis, "Decoding Gobekli Tepe," 233–50.

5. Norris and Harney, "Songlines and Navigation."

6. Malaspinas et al., "A Genomic History of Aboriginal Australia," 207–14.

7. Rito et al., "A Dispersal of *Homo sapiens*."

8. Mountford, *Nomads of the Australian Desert*.

9. Sweatman and Coombs, "Decoding European Palaeolithic Art."

10. Henley, Rossano, and Kardas, eds., *Handbook of Cognitive Archaeology*.

11. Dietrich, Dietrich, and Notroff, "Anthropomorphic Imagery at Göbekli Tepe."

12. Meskell et al., "Figured Lifeworlds and Depositional Practices."

13. Boz and Hager, "Intramural Burial Practices," 413–40.

14. Haddow and Knüsel, "Skull Retrieval and Secondary Burial Practices," 52–71.

15. Palaver, "Death in Çatalhöyük," 41–59.

16. Joan, "Synthesis of the Spiritual Dark-Motherline."

17. Marcuson, "'Word of the Old Woman.'"

18. Warbinek, "The munus.meššu.gi and the kin Oracle," 111–20.

19. Becking and Barstad, "Prophecy and Prophets in Stories."

20. Dijkstra, "Prophets, Men of God, Wise Women."

21. Enoch, "History of Mirrors," 775–81.

22. Speak, "An Odd Kind of Melancholy," 191–206.

PHASE THREE. DREAM WRITING AND RITUAL

1. Etzelmüller and Welker, eds., *The Genesis of Normativity*, 119–35.
2. Reiner, "Astral Magic in Babylonia," i–150.
3. Kokocińska-Kusiak et al., "Canine Olfaction," 2463.
4. Livingstone, "The Isin 'Dog House' Revisited," 54–60.
5. Altman, "Banned Birds."
6. Singh, "Medicinal Leech Therapy (Hirudotherapy)," 213–15.
7. Teall, "Medicine and Doctoring in Ancient Mesopotamia."
8. Finkel, *The Ark Before Noah*, 57.
9. Reiner, *Šurpu*.
10. Hunger and Pingree, "Astronomy."
11. Mikles and Laycock, "Tracking the Tulpa," 87–97.
12. Levene and Bohak, "Divorcing Lilith," 197–217.

PHASE FOUR. TEMPLE SLEEP AND DREAM SANCTUARIES

1. Novak, "Division of the Self," 143–89.
2. Wickens, "A History of the Brain."
3. Szpakowska, "Altered States," 230.
4. Prada, "Dream Books, Ancient Egypt," 1–3.
5. Szpakowska, "Dream Interpretation in the Ramesside Age," 509–17.
6. Matić, "On Typhon," 19.
7. Prada, 2.
8. Szpakowska, "Nightmares in Ancient Egypt," 30.
9. Szpakowska, "Striking Cobra Spitting Fire."
10. Ray, "Observations on the Archive of Ḥor," 113–20.
11. Renberg, "Incubation at Saqqâra," 652.
12. Vaelske, "Coroplastic Figural Art in Egypt."
13. Plaza-Gainza, "Democratizing Dionysus."
14. Gnuse, "Dreams in the Ancient World."
15. Translation by S. R. K. Glanville, as reported by Bevan, House of Ptolemy, 348.
16. Renberg, "Amenhotep and Imhotep."
17. Goldsmith, "Smellscapes in Ancient Egypt," 636–62.
18. Blease, *Sensual Love Poems*, 3.

PHASE FIVE. ISLAND DREAMS

1. Moody et al., "Environmental Archaeology of Prehistoric NW Crete," 273–97.
2. Marinatos, "Sir Arthur Evans and Minoan Crete."
3. Drineas et al., "Genetic History of the Population of Crete," 373–88.
4. Peatfield and Morris, "Dynamic Spirituality on Minoan Peak Sanctuaries," 239.
5. Håland, "The Dormition of the Virgin Mary on the Island of Tinos," 89.
6. Banou, "Minoan 'Horns of Consecration' Revisited," 34.
7. Downey, "Orientations of Minoan Buildings on Crete," 9–20.
8. Ridderstad, "Evidence of Minoan Astronomy and Calendrical Practices," 18.
9. Belmonte, "Finding Our Place in the Cosmos," 35.
10. Ridderstad, 21.
11. "Demeter," New World Encyclopedia website, accessed August 17, 2022.
12. Keller, "The Eleusinian Mysteries of Demeter and Persephone."
13. Behn, "The Use of Opium in the Bronze Age," 194.
14. Behn, "The Use of Opium in the Bronze Age," 195–96.
15. Ramoutsaki et al., "The Snake as the Symbol." 306–8.
16. Håland, "Saints, Snakes, and Healing," 111.
17. Ramoutsaki et al., "The Snake as the Symbol," 306–8.

PHASE SIX. DREAM PANACEA

1. Thompson, "Healing at the Pool of Bethesda," 65–84.
2. Ehrenheim, "Causal explanation of disease in the iamata of Epidauros," 101–18.
3. Martzavou, "Dream, Narrative and the Construction of Hope," 178.
4. Gee, *Mapping the Afterlife,* 230.
5. Pausanias, *Description of Greece,* 1.34.5.

PHASE SEVEN. DREAMS OF THE FUTURE

1. Asarnow, McGlinchey, and Harvey, "The Effects of Bedtime and Sleep Duration," 350–56.
2. Chaput, Dutil, and Sampasa-Kanyinga, "Sleeping Hours," 421–30.
3. Jean-Baptiste et al.," Eye Movement Patterns."

4. Shapiro, "The Role of Eye Movement Desensitization," 71–77.

5. Feinstein, Krippner, and Granger, "Mythmaking and Human Development," 23–50.

6. Oldis, Daniel. "Can We Turn Our Dreams Into Watchable Movies?"

7. Konkoly et al., "Scientists Demonstrate Two-Way Communication."

8. Hearne, "Effects of Performing Certain Set Tasks," 259–62.

9. Berger, "What Causes Muscle Atonia," 1477–78.

10. Hearne, "Dream Machine."

11. Voss et al., "Lucid Dreaming," 1191–200.

12. Edelman and Tononi, *A Universe of Consciousness*.

13. Voss et al., "Induction of Self Awareness in Dreams," 810–12.

14. Schredl et al., "Information Processing During Sleep," 285–90.

15. Soga and Gaston, "Shifting Baseline Syndrome."

16. Costa et al., "Altered States of Consciousness," 135–41.

17. Wise, Frangos, and Komisaruk, "Brain Activity Unique to Orgasm in Women," 1380–91.

Bibliography

Altman, Peter. "Banned Birds: The Birds of Leviticus 11 and Deuteronomy." ("Verbotene Vögel. Die Vögel in Levitikus 11 und Deuteronomium.") *Archaeology and Bible* 1: Tübingen: Mohr Siebeck. 2019.

Artemidorus. *Interpretation of Dreams (Oneirocritica).* Peter Thonemann. ed., Martin Hammond (translator). Oxford, UK: Oxford University Press. 2020

Asarnow, L. D., E. McGlinchey, and A. G. Harvey. "The Effects of Bedtime and Sleep Duration on Academic and Emotional Outcomes in a Nationally Representative Sample of Adolescents." *Journal of Adolescent Health* 54 no. 3 (2014): 350–56.

Aubert, M., P. Setiawan, A. A. Oktaviana, A. Brumm, P. H. Sulistyarto, and E. W. Saptomo. "Palaeolithic Cave Art in Borneo." *Nature* 564 (2018): 254–57.

Badham, Bernard Paul. *Reading Hieroglyphs and Ancient Egyptian Art.* Createspace Independent Publishing Platform, 2016.

Baird, B., A. Castelnovo, O. Gosseries, and G. Tononi. "Frequent Lucid Dreaming Associated with Increased Functional Connectivity between Frontopolar Cortex and Temporoparietal Association Areas." *Scientific Reports* 8, 17798 (2018).

Banou, Emilia. "Minoan 'Horns of Consecration' Revisited: A Symbol of Sun Worship in Palatial and Pre-Palatial Crete?" *Mediterranean Archaeology and Archaeometry,* Vol. 8, No. 1 (2008) Pages 27–47.

Bar-Yosef, O., and F. Valla. "The Natufian Culture and the Origin of the Neolithic in the Levant." *Current Anthropology* 31, no. 4 (1990): 433–36.

Barnstone, Willis, trans. *The Complete Poems of Sappho.* Boulder: Shambhala Publications Inc., 2009.

Becker, C. Beuger, B. Müller-Neuhof, eds., *Iconography and Symbolic Meaning of the Human in Near Eastern Prehistory.* Workshop Proceedings 10th ICAANE in Vienna, Harrassowitz Verlag. Wiesbaden.

Becking, B., and H. M. Barstad (Eds.). "Prophecy and Prophets in Stories." Papers Read at the Fifth Meeting of the Edinburgh Prophets Network Utrecht, October 2013 (OTS, 65), Leiden/Boston: 2015.

Bégouen, C. "The Magic Origin of Prehistoric Art." *Antiquity* 3, no. 9 (1929): 5–19.

Behn, C. Pedro. "The Use of Opium in the Bronze Age in the Eastern Mediterranean." *Listy Filologické/Folia Philologica* 109, no. 4 (1986): 197, I–III,

Belmonte, Juan Antonio, Ph.D., "Finding Our Place in the Cosmos: The Role of Astronomy in Ancient Cultures," in John McKim Malville and Jarita C Holbrook, eds., *Journal of Cosmology* 9, (2010), 2052–2062.

Berger, A J. "What Causes Muscle Atonia in REM?" *Sleep* 31, no. 11 (2008): 1477–78.

Berlucchi G., and H. A. Buchtel. "Neuronal Plasticity: Historical Roots and Evolution of Meaning." *Experimental Brain Research* 192 (2009): 307–19.

Berns, G. S., K. Blaine, M. J. Prietula, and B. E. Pye. "Short- and Long-Term Effects of a Novel on Connectivity in the Brain." *Brain Connectivity* 3, no. 6 (2013): 590–600.

Betz, Hans Dieter. "The Greek Magical Papyri in Translation, Including the Demotic Spells: Texts v. 1." Chicago: University of Chicago Press, 1997.

Bevan, E. R. *The House of Ptolemy: A History of Hellenistic Egypt under the Ptolemaic Dynasty.* London: Methuen Publishing, 1927.

Blease, Kathleen. *Sensual Love Poems.* New York: Ballantine Books, 2002.

Boz, Başak and Lori Hager. "Living above the Dead: Intramural Burial Practices at Çatalhöyük." In *Humans and Landscapes of Çatalhöyük: Reports from the 2000–2008 Seasons.* Los Angeles: Cotsen Institute of Archaeology, 2013.

Burgoyne, Thomas H. *The Light of Egypt; Or, the Science of the Soul and the Stars.* Mansfield Center, Conn.: Martino Fine Books, 2013.

Campbell, Joseph. *The Hero with a Thousand Faces* (The Collected Works of Joseph Campbell). San Francisco: New World Library, 2012.

Chaput, J. P., C. Dutil, and H. Sampasa-Kanyinga. "Sleeping Hours: What Is the Ideal Number and How Does Age Impact This?" *Nature and Science of Sleep* 10 (Nov. 2018): 421–30.

Clinton, Kevin. "Epiphany in the Eleusinian Mysteries." *Illinois Classical Studies* 29 (2004): 85–109.

Costa, R. M., J. Pestana, D. Costa, and M. Wittmann. "Altered States of Consciousness Are Related to Higher Sexual Responsiveness." *Conscious Cogn* 42 (May 2016): 135–41.

Dalley, Stephanie. *Myths from Mesopotamia Creation, the Flood, Gilgamesh, and Others* Oxford, UK: Oxford University Press, 2008.

Dalton, R. "Lion Man Takes Pride of Place as Oldest Statue." *Nature* 425, 7. (2003).

Darvill, T. (2022). "Keeping Time at Stonehenge." *Antiquity,* Vol. 96 (386), 319–35. 1–17.

David, Rosalie. *Religion and Magic in Ancient Egypt.* New York: Penguin, 2002.

Dawes, A. J., R. Keogh, T. Andrillon, and J. Pearson. "A Cognitive Profile of Multi-Sensory Imagery, Memory and Dreaming in Aphantasia." *Scientific Reports* 10, 10022 (2020).

Dietrich, O., L. Dietrich, and J. Notroff. "Anthropomorphic Imagery at Göbekli Tepe." In J. Becker, C. Beuger, B. Müller-Neuhof, eds., *Iconography and Symbolic Meaning of the Human in Near Eastern Prehistory.* Workshop Proceedings 10th ICAANE in Vienna, Harrassowitz Verlag. Wiesbaden. (Forthcoming.)

Downey, William. "Orientations of Minoan Buildings on Crete May Indicate the First Recorded Use of the Compass." *Mediterranean Archaeology and Archaeometry* 11 (2011): 9–20.

Dresler, Martin, , Renate Wehrle, Victor I. Spoormaker, Stefan P. Koch, Florian Holsboer, Axel Steiger, et al. "Neural Correlates of Dream Lucidity Obtained from Contrasting Lucid versus Non-Lucid REM Sleep: A Combined EEG/fMRI Case Study." *Sleep* 35, no. 7 (July 2012): 1017–20.

Drineas, P., F. Tsetsos, A. Plantinga, I. Lazaridis, E. Yannaki, A. Razou, K. Kanaki, et al. "Genetic History of the Population of Crete. *Ann Hum Genet* 83, no. 6 (2019): 373–88.

Edelman, G. M., and G. Tononi. *A Universe of Consciousness.* New York: Basic Books, 2000.

Elce, Valentina, Giacomo Handjaras, and Giulio Bernardi. "The Language of Dreams: Application of Linguistics-Based Approaches for the Automated Analysis of Dream Experience." *Clocks & Sleep* 3, no. 3 (2021): 495–514.

Ehrenheim, Hedvig von. "Causal explanation of disease in the *iamata* of Epidauros," *Kernos* 32 (2019): 101–18.

Enoch, Jay. "History of Mirrors Dating Back 8000 Years." *Optometry and Vision Science* 83 (2006): 775–81.

Etzelmüller, Gregor, and Welker, Michael, eds. *The Genesis of Normativity in Biblical Law, Concepts of Law in the Sciences, Legal Studies, and Theology.* RPT 72, Tübingen: Mohr Siebeck (2013): 119–35.

Feinstein, David, Stanley Krippner, and Dennis Granger. "Mythmaking and Human Development." *Journal of Humanistic Psychology* 28, no. 3 (July 1988): 23–50.

Finkel, Irving. *The Ark Before Noah*. London: Hodder & Stoughton, 2014.

Finkel, Irving, and Jonathan Taylor. "Cuneiform: Ancient Scripts." J. Paul Getty Museum, 2015.

Frazer, James. *The Golden Bough: A Study in Religion and Magic*. Mineola, N.Y.: Dover Publications Inc., 2003.

Freud, Sigmund. *The Interpretation of Dreams*. A. A. Brill, translator. Hertfordshire, UK: Wordsworth Editions Limited, 1997.

Gehring, W., and M. Rosbash. "The Coevolution of Blue-Light Photoreception and Circadian Rhythms." *J Mol Evol* 57, S286–S289 (2003).

Gnuse, R. K. "Dreams in the Ancient World." In *Dreams and Dream Reports in the Writings of Josephus*. Leiden, The Netherlands: Brill, 1996.

Goldsmith, Dora. "Smellscapes in Ancient Egypt." In Kiersten Neumann and Allison Thomason, eds., *The Routledge Handbook of the Senses in the Ancient Near East*. New York: Routledge., 2022.

Grabbe, L. L., and M. C. Korpel, eds. (2015). "Introduction." In *Open-Mindedness in the Bible and Beyond: A Volume of Studies in Honour of Bob Becking* (The Library of Hebrew Bible/Old Testament Studies.) London: Bloomsbury T&T Clark, xi–xxxvi. Retrieved April 10, 2022.

Green, Celia. *Lucid Dreams*. London: Hamish Hamilton, 1968.

Grosman, L., N. D. Munro, and A. Belfer-Cohen. "A 12,000-Year-Old Shaman Burial from the Southern Levant (Israel)." *Proceedings of the National Academy of Sciences of the United States of America*, 105, no. 46 (2008): 17665–669.

Haddow, Scott, and Christopher Knüsel. "The Dormition of the Virgin Mary on the Island of Tinos: A Performance of Gendered Values in Greece." *Journal of Religious History, Vol. 36, No. 1* (2012), 89-117.

———."Skull Retrieval and Secondary Burial Practices in the Neolithic Near East: Recent Insights from Çatalhöyük, Turkey." *Bioarchaeology International* 1 (2017): 52–71.

Håland, Evy Johanne. "The Dormition of the Virgin Mary on the Island of Tinos: A Performance of Gendered Values in Greece." *Journal of Religious History*, Vol. 36, No. 1 (2012), 89–117.

———. "Saints, Snakes and Healing in Modern and Ancient Greece and Italy." *Performance and Spirituality*, Vol. 2, No. 1 (2011).

Hall, Manly P. *Secret Teachings of All Ages: An Encyclopedic Outline of Masonic, Hermetic, Qabbalistic and Rosicrucian Symbolical Philosophy*. New York: Jeremy P Tarcher, 2004.

Hao, Chen, Lai Kaisheng, He Lingnan, Yu Rongjun. "Where You Are Is Who You Are? The Geographical Account of Psychological Phenomena." *Front Psychol* 24 (March 2020).

Hearne, Keith M. T. *Dream Machine*. Detroit: Aquarian Press, 1990.

———."Effects of Performing Certain Set Tasks in the Lucid Dream State." *Perceptual and Motor Skills* 54 (1982): 259–62.

———. *Visions of the Future: An Investigation of Premonitions*. Detroit: Aquarian Press, 1989.

Helle, Sophus. *Gilgamesh: A New Translation of the Ancient Epic*. New Haven, Conn.: Yale University Press, 2022.

Henley, Tracy B., Matt J. Rossano, and Edward P. Kardas, eds. *Handbook of Cognitive Archaeology*. Oxfordshire, UK: Routledge, 2020.

Henshilwood, Christopher, Francesco d'Errico, Karen L. Van Niekerk, Yvan Coquinot, Zenobia Jacobs, Stein-Erik Lauritzen, Michel Menu, and Renata García-Moreno "A 100,000-Year-Old Ochre-Processing Workshop at Blombos Cave, South Africa." *Science* 334 (2011): 219–22.

Hunger, Hermann, and David Pingree. "Astronomy." In *Astral Sciences in Mesopotamia*. Leiden, The Netherlands: Brill, (1999).

Joan, Eahr Amelia. "Synthesis of the Spiritual Dark-Motherline, Integral Research, Labyrinth Learning, and Eco-Thealogy." Re-Genesis Encyclopedia, part 1. Revised Edition 2, 2018. CIIS Library Database.

Johnsen, S., and K. Lohmann. "The Physics and Neurobiology of Magnetoreception. *Nat Rev Neurosci* 6, (2005): 703–12.

Jung, C. G. *The Archetypes and the Collective Unconscious (Collected Works of C. G. Jung)*. Oxfordshire, UK: Routledge, 1991.

———. *Memories, Dreams, Reflections: An Autobiography*. New York: Fontana Press, 1995.

Karp, St. John. *The Ancient Egyptian Book of Dreams*. San Francisco: Remora House, 2016.

Keller, Mara Lynn. "The Eleusinian Mysteries of Demeter and Persephone: Fertility, Sexuality, and Rebirth." *Journal of Feminist Studies in Religion* 4, no. 1 (1988): 27–54.

Kenny, Gavin G., William R. Hyde, Michael Storey, Adam A. Garde, Martin J. Whitehouse, Pierre Beck, Leif Johansson, et al. "A Late Paleocene Age for Greenland's Hiawatha Impact Structure. *Science Advances* 8, no. 10 (2022).

Kingsley, Peter. *Ancient Philosophy, Mystery, and Magic: Empedocles and Pythagorean Tradition*. Oxford, UK: Oxford University Press, 1997.

———. *Reality*. London, UK: Catafalque Press, 2020.

Knitter, Daniel, Ricarda Braun, Lee Clare, Moritz Nykamp, and Brigitta Schütt. "Göbekli Tepe: A Brief Description of the Environmental Development in the Surroundings of the UNESCO World Heritage Site." *Land* 8 (2019).

Kokocińska-Kusiak, A., M. Woszczyło, M. Zybala, J. Maciocha, K. Barłowska, and M. Dzięcioł. "Canine Olfaction: Physiology, Behavior, and Possibilities for Practical Applications." *Animals* 11, no. 8 (2021): 2463.

Konkoly, Karen R., Kristoffer Appel, Emma Chabani, Anastasia Mangiaruga, Jarrod Gott, Remington Mallett, Bruce Caughran, et al. "Real-time dialogue between experimenters and dreamers during REM sleep." *Current Biology*, published online February 18, 2021.

Kraehenmann R. "Dreams and Psychedelics: Neurophenomenological Comparison and Therapeutic Implications." *Curr Neuropharmacol* 15, no. 2 (2017): 1032–42.

Krippner, Stanley and David Feinstein. *Personal Mythology: Psychology of Your Evolving Self Using Ritual, Dreams and Imagination to Discover Your Inner Story*. San Rafael, Calif.: Mandala, 1989.

LaBerge, Stephen. *Exploring the World of Lucid Dreams*. New York: Ballantine Books, 1994.

Lakhovsky, Georges. *The Secret of Life: Cosmic Rays and Radiations of Living Beings*. Mansfield Centre, Conn.: Martino Fine Books, 2013.

Larsen, Clark Spencer. "The Agricultural Revolution as Environmental Catastrophe: Implications for Health and Lifestyle in the Holocene." *Quaternary International* 150, no. 1 (2006): 12–20.

Leschziner, Guy. *The Nocturnal Brain: Nightmares, Neuroscience and the Secret World of Sleep*. New York: Simon & Schuster, 2019.

Levene, Dan, and Gideon Bohak. "Divorcing Lilith: From the Babylonian Incantation Bowls to the Cairo Genizah." *Journal of Jewish Studies* 63 (2012): 197–217.

Livingstone, A. "The Isin 'Dog House' Revisited." *Journal of Cuneiform Studies* 40, no. 1 (1988): 54–60.

Loddo, G., R. Lopez, R. Cilea, Y. Dauvilliers, and F. Provini. "Disorders of Arousal in Adults: New Diagnostic Tools for Clinical Practice." *Sleep Science Practice* 3, no. 5 (2019), https://sleep.biomedcentral.com/articles/10.1186/s41606-019-0037-3.

MacDonald, George. *Lilith*. New York: Ballantine Books, 1895.

Malaspinas, Anna-Sapfo, Michael C. Westaway, Craig Muller, Vitor C. Sousa, Oscar Lao, Isabel Alves, Anders Bergström, et al. "A Genomic History of Aboriginal Australia." *Nature* 538 (2016): 207–14.

Malinowski, Josie. *The Psychology of Dreaming (The Psychology of Everything)*. Oxforshire, UK: Routledge, 2020.

Maranci, Jean-Baptiste, Milan Nigam, Luc Masset, Eva-Flore Msika, Marie Charlotte Vionnet, Charlotte Chaumereil, et al. "Eye Movement Patterns Correlate with Overt Emotional Behaviours in Rapid Eye Movement Sleep." *Scientific Reports* 12, no. 1 (2022).

Marcuson, Hannah. "'Word of the Old Woman': Studies in Female Ritual Practice in Hittite Anatolia." University of Chicago. 2016 dissertation.

Marinatos, Nanno. *Sir Arthur Evans and Minoan Crete: Creating the Vision of Knossos*. New York: Bloomsbury Publishing, 2020.

Martzavou, Paraskevi . "Dream, Narrative and the Construction of Hope in the 'Healing Miracles' of Epidauros" in Angelos Chaniotis (ed.), *Unveiling Emotions: Sources and Methods for the Study of Emotions in the Greek World*, Stuttgart: Franz Steiner Verlag, 2012, 177–204.

Matić, Uroš. "On Typhon, Red Men and the Tomb of Osiris: Ancient Interpretations and Human Sacrifice in Egypt" In *Pervading Empire*, Mihajlovic V, Jankovic M (Eds.) Stuttgart: Franz Steiner Verlag, 2020, 15–28.

McNamara, Patrick. *The Neuroscience of Sleep and Dreams (Cambridge Fundamentals of Neuroscience in Psychology)*. England: Cambridge University Press, 2019.

Meier, C. A. *Healing Dream and Ritual: Ancient Incubation and Modern Psychotherapy*. Einsiedeln, Switzerland: Daimon Verlag, 2009.

Meskell, Lynn, Carolyn Nakamura, Rachel King, and Shahina Farid. "Figured Lifeworlds and Depositional Practices at Çatalhöyük." *Cambridge Archaeological Journal* 18 (2008): 139–61.

Mikles, Natasha L., and Joseph P. Laycock. "Tracking the Tulpa: Exploring the 'Tibetan' Origins of a Contemporary Paranormal Idea." *Nova Religio: The Journal of Alternative and Emergent Religions* 19, no. 1 (2015): 87–97.

Moody, Jennifer, Oliver Rackham, and George Rapp, Jr. "Environmental Archaeology of Prehistoric NW Crete." *Journal of Field Archaeology* 23, no. 3 (1996): 273–97.

Mountford, Charles. *Nomads of the Australian Desert*. Adelaide, Australia: Rigby, 1976.

Murchie, T. J., A. J. Monteath, M. E. Mahony, G. S. Long, S. Cocker, T. Sadoway, E. Karpinski, et al. "Collapse of the Mammoth-Steppe in Central Yukon as Revealed by Ancient Environmental DNA." *Nature Communications* 12, 7120 (2021).

Noegel, S. "Dreams and Dream Interpreters in Mesopotamia and in the Hebrew Bible [Old Testament]." In Bulkeley, K. ed., *Dreams.* New York: Palgrave Macmillan, 2001.

Noegel, Scott, and Kasia Szpakowska. "'Word Play' in the Ramesside Dream Manual." *Studien zur Altägyptischen Kultur* (2006): 193–212.

Norris, Ray, and Bill Harney. "Songlines and Navigation in Wardaman and Other Australian Aboriginal Cultures." *Journal of Astronomical History and Heritage,* Volume 17, Issue 2 (2014).

Novak, P. "Division of the Self: Life After Death and the Binary Soul Doctrine." *Journal of Near-Death Studies* 20 (2002): 143–89.

Oldis, Daniel. "Can We Turn Our Dreams Into Watchable Movies?" *The Huffington Post,* 2016.

———. *The Lucid Dream Manifesto. Reprint of Lucid Dreams, Dreams and Sleep: Theoretical Constructions.* Bloomington, Indiana: iUniverse, 1974.

Palaver. "Death in Çatalhöyük." In I. Hodder, ed., *Violence and the Sacred in the Ancient Near East: Girardian Conversations at Çatalhöyük.* Cambridge: Cambridge University Press, 2019, 41–59.

Patel, A. K., V. Reddy, and J. F. Araujo. *Physiology, Sleep Stages.* StatPearls. Treasure Island, Fla.: StatPearls Publishing, 2022.

Pausanias. *Description of Greece.* Gregory Nagy (trans., ed.) Harvard Center for Hellenic Studies website.

Peatfield, Alan, A. D., and Christine Morris. "Dynamic Spirituality on Minoan Peak Sanctuaries." In Kathryn Roundtree, Christine Morris, Alan A. D. Peatfield, eds., *Archaeology of Spiritualities.* New York: Springer, 2012, 227–45.

Plaza-Gainza, Belen. "Democratizing Dionysus: The Origins Controversy and the Dual Evolution of Tragedy and Civism." Honors Thesis, 2015.

Prada, Luigi. "Dream Books, Ancient Egypt." *The Encyclopedia of Ancient History* (2019): 1–3.

———. "Dreams, Rising Stars, and Falling Geckos: Divination in ancient Egypt." *Egyptian Archaeology* 51 (2017), 4–9.

Price-Williams, Douglass, and Rosslyn Gaines. "The Dreamtime and Dreams of Northern Australian Aboriginal Artists." *Ethos* 22, no. 3 (1994): 373–88.

Ramoutsaki, I. A., S. Haniotakis, and A. M. Tsatsakis. "The Snake as the Symbol of Medicine, Toxicology and Toxinology." *Veterinary and Human Toxicology.* 42, no. 5 (Oct. 2000): 306–8. PMID: 11003127.

Ray, J. D. "Observations on the Archive of Hor." *The Journal of Egyptian Archaeology* 64 (1978): 113–20.

Reiner, Erica. "Astral Magic in Babylonia." *Transactions of the American Philosophical Society* 85, no. 4 (1995): i–150.

———. *Šurpu. A Collection of Sumerian and Akkadian Incantations.* Vienna, Archiv fur Orientforschung, Beiheft 11. (Institute of Oriental Studies, Supplement 11.) 1958.

Renberg, Gill H. "Amenhotep and Imhotep at Deir el-Bahari and Thebes." In *Where Dreams May Come.* Leiden, The Netherlands: Brill, 2017.

———. "Incubation at Saqqâra," in *Proceedings of the Twenty-Fifth International Congress of Papyrology, Ann Arbor 2007.* Trianos Gagos, ed., Ann Arbor: University of Michigan Library, 2010: 649–62.

Ribi, Alfred. *The Search for Roots: C. G. Jung and the Tradition of Gnosis.* Los Angeles: Gnosis Archive Books, 2013.

Ridderstad, Marianna. "Evidence of Minoan Astronomy and Calendrical Practices." Preprint. Arxiv.org, Cornell University. Uploaded October 26, 2009.

Rito, T., D. Vieira, M. Silva, E. Conde-Sousa, L. Pereira, P. Mellars, M. B. Richards, and P. Soares. "A Dispersal of *Homo sapiens* from Southern to Eastern Africa Immediately Preceded the Out-of-Africa Migration." *Scientific Reports* 9, 4728 (2019).

Rochberg, Francesca. "Personifications and Metaphors in Babylonian Celestial Omina." *Journal of the American Oriental Society* 116, no. 3 (1996): 475–85.

Rossini, Stephane, and Shumann-Antelme. *Becoming Osiris: The Ancient Egyptian Death Experience.* Rochester, Vt., Inner Traditions, 2000.

Sacks, Oliver. *Hallucinations.* London: Picador, 2013.

Sandu, A., and Nistor, P. (2020). "Digital Dementia." *Eastern-European Journal of Medical Humanities and Bioethics,* 4(1), 01-06.

Scarpelli, Serena, Chiara Bartolacci, Aurora D'Atri, Maurizio Gorgoni, and Luigi De Gennaro. "The Functional Role of Dreaming in Emotional Processes." *Frontiers in Psychology* 10 (2019).

Schredl, Michael, Desislava Atanasova, Karl Hörmann, Joachim T. Maurer, Thomas Hummel, and Boris Stuck. (2009). "Information Processing During Sleep: The Effect of Olfactory Stimuli on Dream Content and Dream Emotions." *Journal of Sleep Research* 18 (2009): 285–90.

Schwaller de Lubicz, Isha. *Her-Bak: Egyptian Initiate.* Rochester, Vt.: Inner Traditions, 1979.

Schwaller de Lubicz, R. A. *The Egyptian Miracle: An Introduction to the Wisdom of the Temple.* Rochester, Vt.: Inner Traditions, 1999.

———. *Symbol and the Symbolic: Ancient Egypt, Science, and the Evolution of Consciousness*. Rochester, Vt.: Inner Traditions, 2000.

———. *The Temple in Man: Sacred Architecture and the Perfect Man*. Rochester, Vt.: Inner Traditions, 1981.

Shapiro, F. "The Role of Eye Movement Desensitization and Reprocessing (Emdr) Therapy in Medicine: Addressing the Psychological and Physical Symptoms Stemming from Adverse Life Experiences." *Perm J* 18, no. 1 (2014): 71–77.

Shapiro, Francine, and Margot Silk Forrest. *EMDR: The Breakthrough "Eye Movement" Therapy for Overcoming Anxiety, Stress, and Trauma*. New York: Basic Books, 1998.

Singer, Itamar. *Hittite Prayers*. Atlanta, Ga.: Society of Biblical Literature, 2002.

Singh, A. P. "Medicinal Leech Therapy (Hirudotherapy): A Brief Overview." *Complement Ther Clin Pract* 16, no. 4 (Nov. 2010): 213–15.

Soga, Masashi, and Kevin Gaston. "Shifting Baseline Syndrome: Causes, Consequences, and Implications." *Frontiers in Ecology and the Environment* 16 (2018).

Spaeth, Barbette, ed. *The Cambridge Companion to Ancient Mediterranean Religions* (Cambridge Companions to Religion). England: Cambridge University Press, 2013, 11–196.

Speak, Gill. "An Odd Kind of Melancholy: Reflections on the Glass Delusion in Europe (1440–1680. *History of Psychiatry* 1, no. 2 (1990): 191–206.

Steiner, Rudolf. *Knowledge of the Higher Worlds and Its Attainment*. Seaside, Oreg.: Rough Draft Printing. 2012.

———. *The Mystery of the Eleusis*. Whitefish, Mont.: Kessinger Publishing, 2010.

Sweatman, M. B., and D. Tsikritsis. "Decoding Gobekli Tepe with Archaeoastronomy: What Does the Fox Say?" *Mediterranean Archaeometry and Archaeology* 17 (2017): 233–50.

Sweatman, Martin, and Alistair Coombs. "Decoding European Palaeolithic Art: Extremely Ancient Knowledge of Precession of the Equinoxes." *Athens Journal of History* 5, no. 1 (2018), 1–30.

Szpakowska, Kasia. "Altered States: An Inquiry into the Possible Use of Narcotics or Alcohol to Induce Dreams in Pharaonic Egypt." in Aayko K. Eyma and Chris J. Bennet, eds., *A Delta-man in Yebu: Occasional Volume of the Egyptologists' Electronic Forum*, no. 1; Boca Raton: Universal Publishers, 2003, 225–37.

———. *Behind Closed Eyes: Dreams and Nightmares in Ancient Egypt*. Swansea, UK: Classical Press of Wales, 2003.

———. "Dream Interpretation in the Ramesside Age." In Mark Collier and Steven Snape, eds., *Ramesside Studies in Honour of K. A. Kitchen* (Qualicum Beach, BC: Rutherford Press), 2011: 509–17.

———."Nightmares in Ancient Egypt," in Jean-Marie Husser, Alice Mouton, eds., *Le cauchemar dans l'Antiquité: Actes des journées d'étude de l'UMR 7044, 15–16 Novembre 2007, Strasbourg.* Paris: Éditions de Boccard, 2010, 21–39.

———. "Striking Cobra Spitting Fire." *Archiv für Religionsgeschichte* 14, no. 1 (2013).

———. *Through a Glass Darkly: Magic, Dreams and Prophecy in Ancient Egypt.* Swansea, UK: Classical Press of Wales, 2006.

Teall, Emily K. "Medicine and Doctoring in Ancient Mesopotamia," *Grand Valley Journal of History* 3, no. 1 (2014).

Thompson, Robin. "Healing at the Pool of Bethesda: A Challenge to Asclepius?" *Bulletin for Biblical Research* 27, no. 1 (2017): 65–84.

Timmermann, C., H. Kettner, C. Letheby, "Psychedelics Alter Metaphysical Beliefs." *Scientific Reports* 11, 22166 (2021).

Trimestigus, Hermes. *The Way of Hermes: New Translations of the "Corpus Hermeticum" and the "Definitions of Hermes Trismegistus to Asclepius."* London: Bristol Classical Press, 2001.

Trubshaw, Bob. *Dream Incubation.* Leicestershire: Heart of Albion Press, 2017.

Vaelske, V. "Coroplastic Figural Art in Egypt during the Late Period (664–332 BC)." In *Iron Age Terracotta Figurines from the Southern Levant in Context.* Leiden, The Netherlands: Brill, 2021.

Vicente, R., M. Rizzuto, C. Sarica, K. Yamamoto, M. Sadr, T. Khajuria, M. Fatehi, et al. "Enhanced Interplay of Neuronal Coherence and Coupling in the Dying Human Brain." *Frontiers in Aging Neuroscience* 14:813531 (2022).

Voss, U., R. Holzman, I. Tuin, and J. A. Hobson. "Lucid Dreaming: A State of Consciousness with Features of Both Waking and Non-Lucid Dreaming." *Sleep* 32, no. 9 (2009): 1191–200.

Voss, Ursula, R. Holzmann, A. Hobson, W. Paulus, J. Koppehele-Gossel, A. Klimke, and M. A. Nitsche. "Induction of Self Awareness in Dreams through Frontal Low Current Stimulation of Gamma Activity." *Nat Neurosci* 17, no. 6 (June 2014): 810–12.

Walker, Matthew. *Why We Sleep. The New Science of Sleep and Dreams.* New York: Penguin, 2018.

Wallis Budge, E. A. *Amulets and Superstitions: The Original Texts with Translations and Descriptions of a Long Series of Egyptian, Sumerian, Assyrian, Hebrew, Christian.* Brattleboro, Vt.: Echo Point Books & Media, 2017.

————. *The Divine Origin of the Craft of the Herbalist* (Kegan Paul Library of Arcana). Oxforshire, UK: Routledge, 2005.

Wallis Budge, E. A., and John Romer. *The Book of the Dead.* New York: Penguin, 2008.

Warbinek, Livio. "The munus.meššu.gi and the kin Oracle: New Perspectives on the Oracle Inquiry." *Altorientalische Forschungen* 44, no. 1 (2017): 111–20.

Wickens, A. P. "A History of the Brain: From Stone Age Surgery to Modern Neuroscience" (1st ed.). *Psychology Press* (2014).

Wise, N. J., E. Frangos, and B. R. Komisaruk. "Brain Activity Unique to Orgasm in Women: An fMRI Analysis." *J Sex Med* 11 (Nov. 14, 2017): 1380–91.

Zadra A., S. Desjardins, and E. Marcotte. "Evolutionary Function of Dreams: A Test of the Threat Simulation Theory in Recurrent Dreams." *Consciousness and Cognition* 15, 2, (2006), 464–469.

Zbusch, Tzvi, and Karel van der Toorn, eds. *Mesopotamian Magic: Textual, Historical and Interpretative Perspectives (Ancient Magic and Divination, 1).* The Netherlands, Brill: 2000.

Index